Frances C. Hoey

Life of Mme. de la Rochefoucauld

duchess of Doudeauville, founder of the Society of Nazareth

Frances C. Hoey

Life of Mme. de la Rochefoucauld
duchess of Doudeauville, founder of the Society of Nazareth

ISBN/EAN: 9783337300425

Printed in Europe, USA, Canada, Australia, Japan

Cover: Foto ©Lupo / pixelio.de

More available books at **www.hansebooks.com**

THE LIFE

OF

MADAME DE LA ROCHEFOUCAULD.

Ballantyne Press.
BALLANTYNE, HANSON AND CO.
EDINBURGH AND LONDON

THE LIFE

OF

MADAME DE LA ROCHEFOUCAULD,

DUCHESSE DE DOUDEAUVILLE,

FOUNDRESS OF THE SOCIETY OF NAZARETH.

Translated from the French

BY

MRS. CASHEL HOEY,

AUTHOR OF "NAZARETH," ETC. ETC.

LONDON: BURNS & OATES.
1878.

[*All rights reserved.*]

The English Version of this Book

Is Inscribed

to

The beloved Memory

of

CHARLOTTE MURRAY STEWART

Child of Mary of Nazareth.

AUTHOR'S DEDICATION.

To the Children of Mary of Nazareth,—

This book is intended for you, dear children, and it offers the noble and saintly woman, who, in founding the Society of Nazareth, had your welfare in view, as an example to you.

As you read these pages, and meditate upon them, you will admire the qualities of their subject; her strength, courage, perseverance, and consistency; and you will observe that she was at the same time gentle, amiable, and sympathetic. You will, no doubt, ardently desire to imitate her virtues; and, because it is possible for you to imitate them, the following history of a life in which everything is beautiful, for everything is pure and true, is dedicated to you.

The Duchesse de Doudeauville carried humility and mortification to a very high degree, but she was always noble and dignified. No one ever kept her place and sustained her rank better than this perfect Christian, this good, devoted, compassionate woman, whose soul was ever prostrate before God, while her life was devoted to the relief of suffering, and her virtues were enhanced by perfect modesty. There was nothing austere in her piety; it might be said that after she had observed the laws of the Church, her penance consisted in self-denial, most gracefully practised, in ministering to the enjoyment of those around her, and in encouraging others to do well. So much zeal, goodness, and wisdom must needs bear fruit in blessings, such as those which sprung up in the path of this devoted servant of God.

May you, dear children, as you read this book, strengthen yourselves in your resolution to be perfectly faithful, in your turn, to the mission which our Lord gives you to fulfil. May you arrive at a fuller comprehension of the importance of that mission. Your influence will be great, if, like the Duchesse de Doudeauville, you have no other ambition than to do good in the sphere in which Providence has placed you; if, rising above the allurements of vanity and futile pleasures, you seek your own happiness in that of others.

I know, dear children, that the word "devotedness" has a pleasant sound to you. You desire to be generous; but do not forget that our common nature is essentially selfish, and that, if we would renounce and conquer self every day, and all day long, we must draw courage to do so from the inexhaustible spring of the DIVINE CHARITY.

OULLINS, *May* 3, 1877.

TABLE OF CONTENTS.

CHAP.		PAGE
	AUTHOR'S DEDICATION,	vii
I.	MADEMOISELLE DE MONTMIRAIL,	1
II.	THE CHRISTIAN IN THE WORLD,	39
III.	THE SERVANT OF GOD IN HER HOME-LIFE,	74
IV.	DURING THE REVOLUTION,	109
V.	COUNSELS TO A DAUGHTER,	166
VI.	THE DEATH OF MADAME DE RASTIGNAC,	225
VII.	QUIET LIFE,	260
VIII.	NAZARETH,	306
IX.	FAMILY HOPES AND SORROWS,	349
X.	REPOSE IN GOD,	379
	NOTES,	410

INTRODUCTION.

THE English version of this little book is published in aid of the Missions of the Congregation of the Ladies of Nazareth among the women and children of the native land of Our Lord and Our Lady. That Sisterhood, which gratefully calls the Duchesse de Doudeauville its foundress, has not failed to accomplish, with rare devotion, energy, and wisdom, the great task of education to which it has been called in France; and its labours have been abundantly blessed, and are as a light and a beacon in that land, where the powers of good and evil wage so unceasing and so close a contest. But always mindful of the holy memories associated with its name, the Congregation of Nazareth has steadfastly, against various and recurring obstacles, maintained for now twenty-five years a painful crusade in the Catholic East, until it has succeeded in establishing its convents and its schools in the heart of the Holy Land—at Nazareth itself, and since, at Cäiffa, at Chaffa-Amar, at St. Jean d'Acre, at Beyrout. The links of its labours have thus been stretched, in the space of a very few years, from the home of Mary and the cradle of Christianity in the primitive and slowly changing East, to the very midst of that effervescent modern civilisation, which would fain believe that it is meant to be the cemetery of the Christian as of all other religions.

At this moment the state and prospects of Christianity in the East is a question that agitates the mind of mankind throughout the whole world to a degree to which there is no comparison since the time of the Crusades. Hitherto the foreign war caused by the action of Bosnia, the civil wars which preceded, accompanied, and have followed that war, has, to the great credit of the Turkish Government and people, in no way affected the general condition of the Catholic Missions in the Asiatic dominions of the Sultan. Indeed, even in Bessarabia and Bulgaria these Missions have not suffered through any change in the policy of the Porte, but only through the changes consequent upon a foreign intervention as hostile to them as to the Government under which they live. No class of the Sultan's subjects has greater cause to fear and dislike the extension of Russian authority, or influence, than those who hold to the communion of Rome; and none look at this moment with greater hope to the intervention of England.

In her report to the committee of the English Society of Nazareth for this year, the Superior General of the Congregation, Madame Vignon, thus refers to the present position of their Mission in the Holy Land :—

"Owing to the protection of Providence, the ordinary course of our work has not been interrupted by the Russo-Turkish war. On several occasions, indeed, the superiors of our establishments at St. Jean d'Acre and at Chaffa-Amar have been in great perplexity,—fearing, on the one hand, that there was foolhardiness in braving the impending danger; and on the other, that the departure of the nuns might prove to be the signal for a rising against the Christians. The latter grave consideration has prevailed; by degrees all our fears have been dispelled, and the Ladies of Nazareth are pursuing their accustomed ministry among the children, the young girls, and the women of the congregations.

"The most pressing obligation now imposed on us is that of remedying the lamentable evils which have resulted from the war. Heavy taxation, deficient harvests, and infectious disease have increased the poverty of the people, and have also increased the number of children who look to us for daily bread as well as for spiritual instruction. Hitherto I have asked for the beneficent aid of the Committee of our English Society of Nazareth for our five establishments in Syria, and for each of the works to which they are devoted, as I had to make up for large deficits caused by the disasters which France sustained in 1870. As, however, I have reason to believe that sufficient help will be afforded by the Work of the Holy Sepulchre at Cologne, and by our collections in France, to enable us to provide for the annual expenses of our free schools, our dispensaries, and our congregations; I am now desirous of placing our Orphanage at Nazareth under the protection of the English Society, and I propose to devote to that work all funds which may be derived from the Society.

"The prompt reponse which was made to our appeal, in the sweet and holy name of Nazareth, for the Catholics of Syria, and especially for those of Galilee, gave us a consoling assurance of sympathy, and we reckon confidently on its continued manifestation. It will be a happy reflection for all those who aid us in our work, that in the humble little town where the Divine Child grew up in grace and obedience, orphan girl-children are saved by them from peril to their faith, and given that sound and solidly Christian education, in which is to be found the only source of happiness for these orphans, and for the East the sole means of regeneration."

It is hoped that this little volume, which well depicts the life of a lady great by her birth and rank, greater by her dignity and fortitude in adversity, greatest of all by her simple piety and zeal for God's glory, may attract attention and sympathy to a cause with which her name as Foundress is indissolubly associated. It is in this hope mainly that its translation has been prepared; and the names of the Ladies who compose the Committee of the Society are accordingly subjoined. Subscriptions and donations, however small, will be thankfully received by the Secretary and Treasurer.

> The MARCHIONESS OF BUTE, *President.*
> The LADY HOWARD OF GLOSSOP, *Vice-President.*
> The COUNTESS OF DENBIGH.
> The LADY HERBERT OF LEA.
> The LADY HERRIES.

The LADY BEAUMONT.
The LADY O'HAGAN.
The LADY ALEXANDER GORDON LENNOX.
The LADY GEORGINA FULLERTON.
The LADY CONSTANCE BELLINGHAM.
The HONBLE. MRS. PEREIRA.
MRS. CASHEL HOEY.
MISS STANLEY.

Secretary and Treasurer—
MRS. WILLIAM LANGDALE,
8 Charles Street, Berkeley Square.

MADAME DE LA ROCHEFOUCAULD,

DUCHESSE DE DOUDEAUVILLE.

CHAPTER I.

MADEMOISELLE DE MONTMIRAIL.

It is with respectful awe that we venture, in the following memoir, to lift the veil from a life rich in spiritual graces which were carefully concealed by holy humility. The Duchesse de Doudeauville so studiously shunned observation, that even her own children and her intimate friends succeeded but rarely, and then with difficulty and as if by surprise, in obtaining a glimpse of the sublime secrets of her soul. Occasionally one of those communications which were so ardently desired would be gained by a preliminary confidence, and the Duchess would reply with similar unreserve, thus unconsciously betraying herself. But in all such instances it was necessary to conceal every sentiment of admiration which would have grieved the speaker's meek and lowly heart.

Thus it happens that we have but scanty details of a long life which, though marked by heavy trial and swept by violent storms, was, nevertheless, always calm and serene, because it was lived out in purity and strength under the eye of God. And even the little that we know of that life cannot be fully revealed, because the heroism, the patience, and the magnanimity which characterised it, are not to be fully comprehended without a knowledge of the wrongs which were inflicted upon the faithful servant of God. Of those wrongs she never spoke.

Benigne Augustine Françoise le Teillier de Louvois de Montmirail was born in Paris on the fourth of June 1764. She was the daughter of the Marquis de Montmirail, a man of much worth, and a distinguished pupil of the Fathers of the Company of Jesus. He had married the widow of the Marquis de Saint Aulaire, formerly Mademoiselle de Bretonvilliers. This alliance, which was a happy one, was of brief duration, for, after having assisted M. de Buffon in the composition of his "Histoire Naturelle," the young Marquis, who was a brilliant soldier, as well as an accomplished scholar, left home to join the army, and died in camp shortly before the birth of his second child. This sad event was a great calamity. All the hopes of the bereaved family now turned towards the expected child, who might prove to be a male heir to the name and the great estates of his ancestors. The natural and legitimate anxiety of all these noble personages is illustrated by an anecdote which is told of the Maréchal d'Estreés. On learning that the birth of the child was hourly expected, he shut himself up in his room, giving the following order to his servants: "If it is a boy, break the doors open; if it is a girl, let me sleep." There was no need to disturb the old warrior's repose; for the Marquise de Montmirail gave birth to a second daughter, who became Madame de Montesquiou.

After this event, the elder of the two children became the most important member of the family. The little girl's noble relatives had indeed sustained a severe disappointment; but if, in the midst of it, they could have foreseen something of her destiny, of her providential mission, how devoutly would they have bent the knee beside the cradle of the consoling angel, the sustainer, the saviour of her family. Everything which the heart of man can desire and this world has to offer seemed to be the birthright of the charming little creature; a brilliant fortune, a princely position, and remarkable beauty. Nothing which could dazzle was wanting to her lot, and there would have been good reason to tremble for her had not the favourite of earth been also elect of Heaven. The gifts of grace were far beyond the endowments of nature in her case; with the earliest rays of her intelligence the love of God penetrated the child's heart. As soon as she could join her little hands and lisp the names of Jesus and Mary, she uttered the words with such fervour and joy that she seemed like an angel in prayer.

She had been dedicated to the Blessed Virgin, whose snow-white uniform she wore. When she was three years old, Madame de Mancini, her grandmother, who wished to give the child her first coloured dress, had a beautiful frock made for her, of pink gauze with silver spangles and fringe, according to the elaborate fashion of the time. The dress was carried to her room with much ceremony, to the admiration of the waiting-women; but the child, far from being delighted, as every one expected, fixed her large black eyes sadly upon the sumptuous garment, and shed tears when they clothed her in it. The livery of the service of Heaven was already dear to her. All day she persisted in asking for her white clothes; and her attendants had to accede to her childish pleading.

One morning her nurse came to dress her, and found her kneeling up in her little bed with a radiant face. "Oh, nurse," she said, "how beautiful it is! let me still look at it! it is heaven! there is the Blessed Virgin! How beautiful! how beautiful! I shall go there some day."

These were signs of predestination. We shall see by what means God fortified the soul which He had chosen for Himself.

The little girl's childhood, which began so fairly, and was so richly endowed with all the gifts of heaven and earth, proved a very sad one. The Marquis de Montmirail, a good, wise man, was not there to watch over his daughters, and the Marquise, though animated by excellent intentions, was not a judicious mother. She was young, handsome, haughty, elegant, and clever; and she had preserved an unsullied reputation, which was a rare and difficult achievement for a woman in her position in those days. She was nobly generous in the administration of her affairs, and very charitable to the poor, to whom she always gave largely, even after the emigration, when her fortune was seriously impaired; but there were strange contradictions in her conduct, only to be explained by defective bringing up in her youth. She came of a Parliamentarian family, and had been reared in Jansenistic principles, nevertheless she surrounded herself with Jesuits. She loved the great world and its pleasures, and at her country-seat she would collect all the people in the neighbourhood, even the peasants, and dance and romp with them all the evening with the simple glee of a child. She considered it her duty to put an end to dancing at ten o'clock; but as she secretly wished to dance until twelve, she put the clocks back two hours; and this little trick she continued to play for a long time before any one betrayed surprise, on returning home, to find the night so far advanced. She always wore a particular dress when going to Confession, and as in those days the seasons were very distinctly marked in matters of attire, the Marquise required four costumes solely devoted to this sacred purpose. On the day before she received Holy Communion, she would fast, and remain in absolute retreat; then, just as she was setting out to Mass, she would turn round, facing her waiting-women, and say to them: "May God forgive you, Mesdemoiselles, as I forgive you." Believing that she had thus fulfilled the precept of charity, she would devoutly approach the Holy Eucharist.

The Marquise was equally eccentric

in her treatment of her children. She took great trouble with them, but her system of education was strict to the point of harshness. From this Mademoiselle de Montmirail suffered more than her sister; the latter, whose disposition was gay and lively, knew how to disarm her mother by a jest; but Augustine, a timid, shy, embarrassed child, was struck dumb by outbursts of temper which she did not understand, and could only weep in silence. The Marquise, taking her daughter's patient resignation as a reproach for her arbitrary conduct, was doubly irritated by her tears. She exaggerated the best systems of education in all respects; thus, for example, she insisted that her children should eat of everything without any exception, and without regard to constitutional peculiarities. On one occasion the younger child was locked up all day with a dish of carrots, and not released until she had eaten them.

Mademoiselle de Montmirail was much beloved by her uncles, her sister, her governesses, and her attendants; and as they treated her with great affection, they consoled her to some extent for the severity of her mother. The Maréchal d'Estreés called her "Bellotte," and her really remarkable beauty might have proved a fatal gift to her, for she heard it incessantly praised. But one day, when she was six years old, she was looking at herself in a mirror, and instead of her own beautiful face a skull met her eyes. Was this the effect of an excited imagination? or was it one of those exceptional graces which Almighty God grants to privileged souls? We cannot venture to decide that question; but it is quite certain that when she was seventy, and again when she was eighty years old, the Duchesse de Doudeauville still spoke with terror of the impression which that image of death had made upon her. From that moment the fear of offending God caused her to regard her beauty as a perilous possession, and this wholesome fear never forsook her, even in the hours of her most brilliant social success.

Each morning their governess took the two little girls to their mother's room while she was dressing. After they had kissed the hand of the Marquise, they learned their lessons in her presence, and they were severely punished if they did not repeat them correctly. Mademoiselle Augustine was only seven years old when she lost her great-uncle, the Maréchal d'Estreés, who loved her dearly. The gallant veteran died like a Christian hero. When they brought him the last Sacraments, he insisted on rising, notwithstanding his acute sufferings, fitly to receive

Our Lord. During this time his greatniece was praying fervently in an adjoining room; she understood that something serious was happening, and that she was losing a friend. She already had deep thoughts of eternity.

The children passed nearly six months of every year at Binanville, one of the family estates near Mantes, under the care of their governess. Thither Madame de Montmirail went frequently to visit them, but her arrival was usually the signal for some punishment or other. And yet Augustine was most diligent in her studies. Her chief happiness consisted in hearing Mass, which was frequently said in the private chapel of the château by an aged Cordelier. The gentle old man remarked the angelic child, and, touched by her piety, would often interpose as a mediator between her and her mother. Among the recollections of her childhood on which the Duchess dwelt with pleasure were the dolls, the walks in a pretty wood, the country cakes, and the milk which the two little girls were given by a certain "Jeannette's mother" at her farm. Thanks to their affection, "Jeannette" was first well educated, and then well married; and they used to take great pleasure in going to see her.

When her daughters were of an age to combine serious studies with accomplishments, the Marquise engaged the best teachers for them. Madame Leprince de Beaumont, who has written several excellent books for the young, gave them lessons for three years. She was much attached to her pupils, and after she had left them and gone to Spain, she wrote affectionately to Mademoiselle Augustine, who was very proud of the correspondence. A pupil of Rollin's replaced this efficient instructress as their teacher of history, and he led the two children to feel a warm interest in their studies. This pious man mingled wise reflections with his lessons, to the great satisfaction of the serious-minded Augustine. He frequently spoke to her of her father, whom she had never known, but whom every one had loved and honoured. It seemed to the child that all who spoke of him meant that had he lived, he would have made his little daughter's life happy. Did this awaken profound regret in her, and suggest a comparison which may be easily divined? We do not know. The dear child never complained, and she accused no one. Long afterwards, when speaking of her childhood, she was reminded that she must have had a great deal to suffer. She said simply — "My mother was a good woman, and if she was hard and severe towards me, I thank God for it as a great favour; for if, in my childhood, I had found a friend in her, with my sensitive and ardent nature, I should have attached myself too strongly to the creature."

It was, then, in order to reserve her young heart entirely to Himself, and to prepare her for the strife to come, that in the morning of life the Lord initiated her into suffering, and revealed to her the secrets of His love.

One day, Madame de Montmirail had her daughter summoned to her presence, and said to her in a tone which admitted of no reply—"You have told a falsehood, Mademoiselle, and you shall quit my house on the spot."

Augustine, whose sole fault was that she had made a hesitating answer to a trifling question, was hurried in utter bewilderment into a carriage, and arrived, before she had at all recovered herself, at the gate of the Convent of the Visitation. She was presented to the nuns as a little culprit; but to their great astonishment they discovered in their new pupil the sweetest, gentlest, and most pious of children, who soon won the affection of them all. At first she grieved much for the loss of her sister, her attendant, and all her surroundings; but by degrees the atmosphere of peace, silence, and the love of God which pervaded the holy house, assuaged her grief, and the convent became a haven in which she enjoyed perfect rest and calm of soul. There too she learned the joys of friendship, for, notwithstanding the absolute difference between their respective dispositions, she became greatly attached to Mademoiselle de Sinetti. They were companions in study and in recreation, and in later days they were companions in the deepest sorrows of maternity. Until an advanced age it was the task of the saintly Duchesse de Doudeauville to sustain and console the brilliant Duchesse de Caderousse, who always regarded her friend with mingled tenderness and veneration.

Mademoiselle de Montmirail remained only six months at the Convent of the Visitation; but her brief sojourn was marked by a great event, whose anniversary she celebrated every year of her life with joy and thankfulness. Time, far from weakening this sentiment, did but strengthen it; for, towards the end of her long life, when her soul seemed to be awakening more and more fully to the things of heaven as indifference towards the things of earth grew upon her, the mere mention of St. John's Day sufficed to thrill her frame and light up her countenance with joy. "Oh!" she would exclaim, "that was the day of my First Communion."

What had passed in the heart of the young girl on that solemn occasion? No doubt God had given her wonderful consciousness and sensible enjoyment of His Presence; for, after she had made a long thanksgiving, and all her companions had left the chapel, Mademoiselle de Montmirail continued to kneel. She saw nothing, she heard nothing, she seemed to be transported into heaven. The nun who was sent to summon her to rejoin the other pupils did not venture to disturb her, but paused respectfully as she beheld the devotion of the child, who was lost in the sense of the presence of God. But, as she still continued in prayer, the nun, fearing the physical exhaustion which might follow, at length decided on summoning her.

"What!" said Augustine, with pained

surprise, "must I go so soon?" and it needed a strong effort of obedience to enable her to rise from her *prie-Dieu*.

After her first communion, Mademoiselle de Montmirail experienced a strong and urgent desire to consecrate herself entirely to the service of God. The convent was full of attraction for her; the calm and regular life which she led there was far more congenial to her disposition than the stress and turmoil of the world; the kindness of her teachers, the friendship of her companions, filled her heart with gladness. Great, therefore, was the trouble into which she was thrown when, on the evening of the happy day of her first communion, her mother informed her that she was immediately to return to the Hôtel de Louvois. For once, and by a great effort, she overcame her habitual timidity, and hazarded a request. "Until this moment," she said, "I have never thought of anything except my first communion; if you will permit me to remain here three or four days longer, in order to prepare myself to go out into the world again, I shall be very grateful."

Madame de Montmirail willingly acceded to the request of her daughter, who continued her retreat with fervour and seriousness far beyond her age. Long afterwards, in one of those rare moments of confidence to which we have alluded, she revealed the impressions of that solemn time.

"All that the world holds dear seemed despicable to me, and I could not understand how any one could care for such things. While I was kneeling, praying with all my heart and soul, in the little gallery of the chapel, I could see the nuns prostrating themselves upon the ground, and remaining for hours together before the Tabernacle; to me they seemed happy beyond all expression, and in my childish enthusiasm I kissed the walls of the cloister, within which I would gladly have lived all the rest of my days. I had a profound love of Saint Francis de Sales, whom I called 'our holy founder;' and so eager became my longing to be numbered among his daughters, that one day, after my meditation, and quite ignorant of the meaning of the obligation, I was about to pronounce the vow of perpetual virginity, when I seemed to hear a voice which said to me distinctly: 'No, in the world, against all thine inclinations.' Then, trembling and weeping, I replied, 'As Thou willest, Lord; but at least grant that the will of my mother may be the expression of Thine.' After this it seemed to me that I should have to practise the virtues of the cloister without tasting any of its consolations, to apply myself to humility of life in an exalted position; to poverty in the midst of wealth; to mortification under the externals of luxury; to the strictest modesty while among the follies and vanities of the age. The sacrifice cost me dear, but I could not entertain any doubt of the will of God, and I besought Him to help me to overcome my repugnance."

When the three days of grace had elapsed, Mademoiselle de Montmirail, now completely resigned, once more assumed the yoke of her mother's severe and capricious rule. The Marquise continued to punish her severely for the most trifling offences, chiefly for slight omissions in matters of etiquette, and for the awkwardness which arose from her timidity. The young girl had an excessive dread of her mother's pitiless glance; it still paralysed her, just as it had done when she was a child; and she was actually, on one occasion, a week before her marriage, ordered by the Marquise to dine alone at a side-table in a corner, because she had made an ungraceful curtsey on entering the drawing-room.

The daily misery of that wretched period of her life commenced in the morning; when the elaborate hairdressing then in fashion had to be gone through. For two mortal hours every day was Mademoiselle de Montmirail's magnificent hair, which she ardently desired to have cut off, under the hands of her maid. She was peculiarly sensitive to pain, and during these two hours she suffered severely. It was her custom to pass the time in meditating in utter stillness on the crowning of our Blessed Lord with thorns.

In the meantime everybody was discussing the question of the marriage of the wealthy and beautiful heiress; she only took no interest in the matter. There was no lack of aspirants to the hand of the young lady, who united remarkable personal attractions to a great fortune and numerous privileges of rank, among which was a grandeeship of Spain of the first class, attached to the dukedom of Doudeauville in the Boulonnais. Who was the happy mortal destined to carry off this prize? Many great names were mentioned, and the claims of all the most distinguished young nobles of the day were discussed. All of a sudden the Vicomte de la Rochefoucauld had himself presented at the Hôtel Louvois, having previously had no acquaintance whatever with Madame de Montmirail. This circumstance caused a great stir in the household of the Marquise. What had the Vicomte come about? Inquiries were made, and it was found that he had only one son, who was still a child. Perhaps he had come on behalf of one of his nephews? Yet surely none of them would be a fitting match for the eldest daughter of the house of Montmirail. It must therefore be on behalf of the son, who was away on his travels, that the Vicomte had come to visit the Marquise. Every one was lost in conjecture except Augustine, who did not know or think anything at all about the matter.

The Vicomte de la Rochefoucauld-Surgères represented one of the younger branches of that illustrious family, which, coming originally from the province of Guienne, is allied with the Dukes of Aquitaine under the Carlovingian dynasty, and with the Sires de Lusignan in the time of the Crusades, when its shield was first blazoned.

The Montendre-Surgères branch commenced in the sixteenth century in the person of Louis de la Rochefoucauld, fifth son of that Duke Francis who had the honour of holding Francis the First at the baptismal font, and of giving his own name to the royal child.

One day, after an unusually elaborate and tedious hairdressing, Mademoiselle de Montmirail's maid presented for her approval a costume which was much more elegant than her customary attire. She asked in some surprise for an explanation.

"Is it possible!" said the waiting-woman, "that Mademoiselle does not know that the Vicomte de la Rochefoucauld is to come here to-day to ask her hand in marriage?"

The young lady made no reply, but, finishing her toilet as rapidly as possible, she went to her mother's room, and throwing herself on her knees before her, said—

"You know that I am unhappily destined to have a great fortune. It is my earnest desire never to leave you, and if I should have the misfortune to survive you, I wish to devote all my possessions to charitable purposes."

"Impossible!" replied the Marquise with icy coldness; "the Vicomte de la Rochefoucauld is about to ask you in marriage for his son, whom he will bring here this evening. Observe him carefully; if he does not suit you, you can tell me so: I will look out for another."

"I need not observe him, mother," said Mademoiselle Montmirail. "If I must indeed marry, let it be he whom you have chosen."

"Very well," said the Marquise with the same indifference, and seemingly unconscious of her daughter's agitation. The poor girl left the presence of her inexorable mother with a full heart indeed, but submissively. She had accepted the sacrifice.

The reception that evening was indeed magnificent; but one may imagine what was the general effect! Mademoiselle Montmirail, splendidly attired, and dazzling with beauty, youth, and grace, found herself in the presence of a little boy who had not yet attained his fourteenth year; a thin, delicate, insignificant child, with babyish features, shy, awkward, and even more vexed than embarrassed by the part which he was made to play. On being told that the matter in hand was the arrangement of a marriage for him, he exclaimed in a melancholy tone, "Ah, then, I shall not be able to amuse myself any more!" The hero and heroine of the evening hardly looked at each other; and when Madame de Montmirail asked her daughter whether the young Ambrose was pleasing to her, she replied, "Just as much so as anybody else."

Then came several formal interviews, during which the future bride and bridegroom did not exchange a word. What must have been in the mind of the serious and thoughtful young girl, whose wisdom so much surpassed her years, as she contemplated the timid, shy, shrinking lad, desperately disconcerted by the premature importance which had been thrust upon him, and thought of him as her future counsellor and guide, as the centre of all her affections? But if she suffered, so did the unfortunate Ambrose, who was afraid to look at her, so overawed was he by her beauty, and especially by her height, and who wondered despondingly whether this wretched state of constraint was to be his condition for the rest of his life.

No dream of happiness, one may see, had any part in this strange alliance. When the young girl set her signature to the most important act of her life, it was in obedience, as she thought, to the command of Heaven; she heard once more those words which had annihilated her dearest hopes: "In the world, against all your inclinations." She accepted her lot, but it was with the resignation of a generous victim. As for the boy of fourteen, when he tremblingly affixed his signature to the solemn contract, it was done in mere obedience to his father, and like any other prescribed penance.

On the 10th of April 1779, the great gates of the Hôtel de Louvois were thrown open, disclosing to view the "Cent-Suisses," in their full-dress uniform, occupying the grand entrance-court; many magnificent carriages and richly caparisoned horses, numerous servants in state liveries with gorgeous bouquets; all the preparations for a festival. Soon, in the midst of a brilliant group, there appeared a beautiful and majestic girl, whose agitation was so great that the orange blossoms on her dress shook like leaves in a breeze. In vain would the hero of the occasion have been sought for among the great nobles and gallant gentlemen who swelled the train of the lovely lady; this part was enacted by a stunted boy, who, however high and rigidly he held up his head, barely reached the shoulder of his bride. The poor little fellow paid rather dearly that day for the honours of the moment and the happiness of the future. All the "Cent-Suisses" were men of six feet high, so that his escort effectually showed off the insignificance of his appearance. Everybody looked at him; he attracted more attention than did his bride, by the mere force of the contrast between them; a preference with which he would most willingly have dispensed.

In those days they laughed at incongruities of this kind; in these, we should be saddened, or at least surprised, by the contemplation of so strange an alliance. Time was destined to prove that the appearances of that day were deceitful; in this instance, at least, the reality was better than the promise. The boy-bridegroom was to become a man truly worthy in all respects of his fortune, his name, and the high functions which he was afterwards to exercise. Upright, kindly, loyal, high-minded, and generous, he was to make his noble wife as happy as it is possible for a soul which aspires only to the Divine union to be made in this world.

Had the illustrious patrons of Augustine and Ambrose inspired this really holy alliance, and blessed it from their high places in heaven? We may be permitted to believe that this was so, when we count the treasures which this lofty-souled and strong-hearted woman amassed for eternity, and the good which she did in her husband's family.

If, on their wedding-day, she could have read the heart of the timid youth who accompanied her to the altar, she would have seen with admiration that, though surrounded by innumerable errors and prejudices, he had preserved the integrity of his faith.

The parents of Ambrose de la Rochefoucauld had lost three sons, and fearing lest the fourth should also be taken from them, they sent him to be nursed in the country when he was only a few days old. Until he had completed his sixth year, the child led a free and healthful life, running about in the fields, and in every kind of weather, breathing pure air all day long. His parents thought of nothing beyond his health, but Providence, solicitous for the salvation and preservation of his soul, placed him in the charge of an excellent nurse. This honest, simple peasant woman, while bestowing upon him every material care, sowed in his soul the seeds of eternal truth. She taught the child his catechism, which he learned with avidity; his lively imagination was fired by her histories of the lives of the saints, and his natural courage led him to desire martyrdom. The pious nurse, who dreaded the atmosphere of incredulity which her nursling, whom she tenderly loved, would have to breathe, and solicitous for the preservation of his faith, used to make him kneel down every morning with his face turned towards the clock-tower of the village church. Then, pointing to it, she would say—

" Look at that cross. Our Lord is there. He can grant us all that we ask Him ; let us pray together, and do you say with me :—My God, grant that my heart may never be corrupted by evil doctrines."

This prayer was so deeply impressed upon the child's memory, that when, many years afterwards, a sceptical tutor, an adherent of the false ideas of the day, endeavoured to infect his pupil with the poison of infidelity, the young man was filled with instinctive fear, and going into his alcove, he knelt down behind the curtains of his bed, and repeated with fervent faith :—" My God, grant that my heart may never be corrupted by evil doctrines." Thanks to this simple petition, he escaped many and grave dangers.

No exchange of speech and sentiment had, however, made known the mind of her bridegroom to the young wife. She entered upon the unknown leaning only upon the Divine will, which she had sought to know, and whence, after the example of her Saviour, she derived all the nourishment of her soul.

The marriage ceremony was performed by the Cardinal de la Rochefoucauld. After a sumptuous wedding-feast, and a magnificent reception in the evening, the young Ambrose, now Duc de Doudeauville, who hailed with joy the conclusion of a day which had brought him no pleasure except that of listening to the drums, set out for Versailles, accompanied by his tutor. The bride of fifteen was handed over to the charge of her mother-in-law, the Vicomtesse de la Rochefoucauld, to continue in her house her former maiden life. Different as was the system of Madame de la Rochefoucauld from that of Madame de Montmirail, it was, as we shall soon see, even less commendable.

CHAPTER II.

THE CHRISTIAN IN THE WORLD.

A NEW life in a new world opened before the charming young woman who, to her great regret, was an object of curiosity and observation to the brilliant and pleasure-loving circle in which she lived. She had passed without any transition stage from the side-table of her publicly-inflicted penance to the sumptuous entertainments of the court. If she was sometimes timid, if all the formal splendour of her life was oppressive to her modest tastes, she was never for a moment dazzled; and as we follow her through the scenes of her "success," as it was called, we shall trace only the triumphs of piety and faith.

The Vicomtesse de la Rochefoucauld, who was very proud of her beautiful daughter-in-law, required her to wear the richest dresses and ornaments during the series of bridal visits which had to be gone through. Society, at that time, was exaggerated in its tone; everybody got up a passion for the idol of the day, and the flame of enthusiasm spread rapidly and rose high; generally, however, its life was ephemeral. The beauty of the young Duchesse de Doudeauville became the topic of the day; to get a sight of her was the object of the multitude; every *salon* in which she was expected was thronged with guests, and when at length she was announced, the lady of the house would give orders, in a loud voice, that the lustres and all the candles should be lighted. The Duchess, blushing at and shrinking from this publicity, would be all the time praying earnestly to God to release her from these perilous honours.

It was the custom among persons of high rank that a bride should be presented to the public, and in compliance with this social rule, the Duchess, accompanied by all the wedding guests, went to the opera; and there, surrounded by her relatives, she advanced, and made a grand court curtsey to the pit and boxes. The house rose at her, and greeted her with such tumultuous and prolonged applause, that after the salutations exacted by etiquette, she hid herself as quickly as possible at the back of her box.

When Madame de la Rochefoucauld presented her daughter-in-law at court, the great gallery of the palace at Versailles was crowded with curious courtiers; they stood up on the chairs and benches to get a good view of her; and a loud buzz of admiration surrounded her as she walked between the ranks of her admirers to the presence chamber. This preliminary trial so much increased her agitation and embarrassment, that, though she was received with the utmost kindness by the King, the Princes, and the Princesses, she was obliged to ask the Queen's leave to absent herself from the royal card-table on that evening. A sharp attack of fever was the result of this brief triumph.

A state quadrille was announced at the court; the Duchess was invited to take part in it, and the invitation was a courteous command which was not to be gainsaid. She had to put aside her natural timidity and her dislike of everything of the kind, and to attend the frequent rehearsals which were indispensable in the case of a court entertainment

to which the whole *beau monde* was looking forward. On these occasions the tone of the frivolous society of the period was anything but edifying; happily, Madame de la Rochefoucauld learned nothing there except the steps of the prescribed dances; her perfect modesty kept the most daring and licentious of the courtiers at a distance, and even scoffers and profligates were forced to admire her propriety of conduct and her purity of mind.

The much-talked-of quadrille was to be danced at Versailles; and the other ladies, all jealous of the young Duchess, who unconsciously and involuntarily eclipsed them all, conspired against her after a fashion which reminds us of the plot against a very different personage, Madame Dubarry. They agreed to engage the services of Leonard, the celebrated court hairdresser, for each of them in advance of the Duchess, and to detain him until the last moment, so that she could not have her hair dressed in time to appear. When we recall what hairdressing meant in the reign of Louis XVI., this plot assumes its due significance to our imagination. The moment arrived, and this petty feminine device was in due process of successful fulfilment. One of the conspirators actually left the others and went to the apartment of the Duchess in order to enjoy the spectacle of her annoyance and anxiety. How great was the surprise and the discomfiture of the malicious visitor when she found the Duchess sitting quietly in her room reciting vespers, for it was Sunday, and totally unconcerned! The lady regained her friends, feeling at once disconcerted and edified against her will. Immediately afterwards Leonard arrived, out of breath, and exclaiming, "Ah, the schemers! the traitresses! they have only left me five minutes; but never mind, your hair shall be as well done as theirs, and better." And Leonard kept his word.

Little did the quiet-minded lady value her triumph, but she was grateful to the loyal hairdresser for his good-will, and she gave him substantial proof of her gratitude.

The success of the entertainment was complete, and while the Vicomtesse de la Rochefoucauld was perfectly intoxicated with pride and delight at the praise and admiration which were showered upon her daughter-in-law, the young Duchess whispered with pious fear, as she kissed her—

"Oh, mother, mother! would you destroy me?"

The grace and loveliness which excited so much admiration alarmed the tender conscience of their possessor. She regarded them as an occasion of sin, and the least yielding to their suggestions filled her with horror. On one single occasion, having overheard it said that her eyes were remarkably beautiful, especially when she looked upwards, she had instinctively raised her eyes to the ceiling; but the next moment, stricken with shame and repentance, she cast down her eyelids, and all her life thenceforth she reproached herself for having allowed vanity to gain such an advantage over her.

On the important occasion of the reception of the Knights of the Order of the Saint Esprit, the young Duchess was selected for the office of *quêteuse,* or collector of the offertory in the chapel at Versailles; and she acquitted herself so well, that shortly afterwards she was again nominated to the same distinction, a proceeding which was contrary to the custom of the court. This innovation occurred on the occasion of the visit of the Emperor Paul I.,* and was due to the King's anxiety that his imperial visitor should form a favourable impression of the French ladies. The Queen sent off an express to the Duchesse de Doudeauville, who was then at Turny, to request her to return to the court, and Her Majesty lent her diamonds to the Duchess for the occasion.

Such was the exterior life of this young woman between her fifteenth and seventeenth years. Let us who know what were her tastes, how true and deep was her piety, glance at her interior life, and see whether, in the privacy of her home and the society of her family, she had any compensation for such trials, or was free to give vent to the aspirations of her soul.

The Hôtel la Rochefoucauld-Surgères,

* See Note A.

the house of the Duchess's father-in-law, was, at that epoch, the chief social centre of the philosophy and wit of the day. There all the fashionable theories were discussed, there all the inventions of intellectual pride and folly were vaunted as new revelations. Philanthropy, allied to indifferentism in religion, took the place of the real and solid virtues which Christianity alone can produce. Pure faith, sacred dogma, were left to the simple-minded and the ignorant, to women and children. Intelligent persons, with strong minds and mature powers of reasoning, were bidden to rest content with a vague, ideal, indefinite notion of something that was neither belief nor worship. The entire family of La Rochefoucauld had adopted these false doctrines, with the sole exception of the young Ambrose. Thus it is easy to understand the trials which awaited one who had joined that family circle, adorned with piety and the grace of God to even a higher degree than with beauty and fascination. Her new relations attacked her faith with jests and sarcasm, and turned her dearest convictions into ridicule. At first she was astonished; she had never conceived the idea that so much impiety existed in the world. To astonishment succeeded acute suffering; this laughter, jesting, and mockery caused her the deepest pain. These people seemed to be always asking her in derision, "Where is your God?" What torment for this devout soul, of whom it might indeed be said, that "the zeal of the House of the Lord had devoured her."

Throughout all the young Duchess kept silence, because, although the blasphemies which she was forced to hear did not tarnish the lustre of her faith in the slightest degree, she would not have been able to defend that faith in words. Her studies had not been sufficiently deep or extensive to enable her to combat arguments if she had been assailed with them. She felt the falsehood of all that was said, but she had sought in religion for light to guide her to the fulfilment of her duties, not to the refutation of doubts which had never occurred to her mind. Her silence was imputed to stupidity; she was well aware that such was the general opinion, and it pained her deeply, but she never appeared conscious of it.

Before her marriage she had stipulated that she was to be permitted to practise her religion in perfect freedom, and had been promised that so it should be. Nevertheless, every day of abstinence was made a day of punishment to her. She was the only person at her father-in-law's table who observed the law of the Church, and each time that she did so, her obedience gave rise to a "scene." In vain did her mother-in-law, who really loved her, endeavour to interpose between her and the Vicomte de la Rochefoucauld; he would promise to keep silence for the future, and then, on the next occasion, begin again to reproach her, now ironically, again angrily, and his mortifying speeches to herself always included sarcasms which pierced the heart of the fervent young Christian. So keen was her dread of this oft-recurring trial, that she frequently passed a great part of the night between Thursday and Friday in prayer. Kneeling before her crucifix, with streaming tears she would implore strength to endure the strife, and when the dreaded meal-time came, she would earnestly recommend herself to God, and go down to the dining-room with a heart beating almost to suffocation. Then she would take her place at table impassive as a marble statue, seeing and hearing nothing.

On entering the family of La Rochefoucauld, the Duchess had made it a condition that she should be permitted to hear Mass daily; but after a short time she was denied this solitary consolation, under the pretext that the horses were overworked. She did not insist, thinking it more wise to restrict herself to exacting that she should be taken to Mass on Sundays and Feasts of Obligation. The prudent and firm attitude which she maintained on this point, gained her the respect of all, and, in the midst of difficulties, she was so happy as never once to have failed in fulfilling a precept of the Church.

The Duchess looked upon theatres as dangerous places of amusement; and earnestly wished to be excused from attending them. She privately implored her mother-in-law to aid her in this matter. Madame de la Rochefoucauld, who sincerely wished to render herself agreeable to her new daughter, had recourse to various subterfuges in order to put off the visits to the theatres, which took place, generally speaking, three times a week. Now she would complain of headache; again she would be too much fatigued just as the time came for her to start, a third and ready excuse was that she did not like the piece which was to be performed. Notwithstanding all these maternal manœuvrings, the young Duchess sometimes found herself obliged to go to a theatre, and on those occasions she looked as she felt, indifferent to the performance which attracted the crowd. Preoccupied by the fear of offending God, she abstracted her mind from what was before her eyes, and so she passed for a young person of very limited intelligence. Her indifference contrasted strongly with the enthusiasm of her companions; and she exhibited the same cold avoidance of the objectionable romances of the day. She was pronounced to be totally devoid of sensibility, a judgment which pained her deeply: "She appreciates nothing, she understands nothing;" such was the verdict of society upon her, and the whispers in which it was pronounced were accompanied by significant glances and pitying smiles. Conversation was interrupted when she appeared, or it was continued with an affectation on the part of the speakers of not knowing that she was in the room. Nothing of all this escaped her notice, and she must have been capable of strong self-control to have endured it without the least appearance of consciousness. She was, in reality, very far from dull or indifferent; every noble and elevated sentiment found a ready echo in her heart, and all deeds of charity had her warmest sympathy.

It was true that the young Duchess avoided reading of a kind which was hurtful to morals and religion, but she took even too much interest in what are called "good" novels. During the first two years after her marriage, she frequently allowed herself to be tempted into reading until very late at night, and on one occasion she was so carried away by the interest of the story, that her table-clock struck four in the morning while she was deep in her book. The strokes sounded a moral alarum for Madame de la Rochefoucauld. She stopped in surprise at her own absorption, and reflected thus:—"If this book is not bad in itself, at all events my time is ill-employed in reading it." She closed the volume, never to reopen it, or any other of a similar kind. From that moment she fed her heart and her intelligence on the simple and solid food of truth only. Much of her time was passed before the Tabernacle, with a little book in which she delighted, and which she counted among her most precious possessions. The Marquis de Montmirail, her father, had had an old school friendship with Alphonsus de Liguori, and she, founding her request upon that highly-prized sentiment, wrote to the zealous apostle of the cultus of Mary and the Holy Eucharist, to implore his prayers and his blessing. His answer, which was accompanied by a copy of "Visits to the Blessed Sacrament," was received with deep and joyful gratitude.

While the Duchess was thus enduring innumerable petty persecutions, the

Duc de Doudeauville had similar opposition to encounter, and he also met it with passive resistance. The following passages are taken from his own Memoirs:—

"Those persons to whom I owed respect and confidence had been giving me, for two years past, some books on Materialism, and the worst of Voltaire's works, in order to 'form' my mind and heart. In addition to this, conversations to the same effect were held in my presence in support of these books; but my teachers had no success, I made no progress in studies of this kind.

"In order to escape from the strange conversations and the dangerous books, which I comprehended perfectly, I used to pretend that I did not understand anything I read or heard. I preferred to be taken for a poor fool rather than to deserve the title of *esprit fort*, which was so much coveted at that time by the young nobility of France. As soon as I could get away, I used to go to my room, and pray to God upon my knees, that He would not suffer the religion which He had placed in my soul to be destroyed. Contentment, submission and happiness came to me, each time that I fulfilled my obligations as a Christian in those days, and ever since it has given me consolation, strength, resignation, and the love of my duty."

The Duc de Doudeauville adds that he went from time to time to see his young wife, but as they were never allowed to meet without witnesses, no exchange of feeling was possible. They tried to make up for this restraint by a correspondence which soon became active, tender, and interesting. Both husband and wife took great, and surely innocent, pleasure in this exchange of thoughts and sentiments, but, all of a sudden, for some inexplicable reason, the De la Rochefoucauld family took alarm at these frequent letters. What could two young people who did not know each other have to say? Was the young Duchess acquiring influence over her husband which would be dangerous, being Christian? In order to make sure on this point, her desk was opened during her absence, and her husband's letters, the innocent source of all her truest pleasure, were taken away. The loss of them gave her the keenest pain.

Notwithstanding all this, her husband's family sincerely desired to render the young Duchess happy. If they opposed her tastes, it was with the intention of increasing her enjoyments; if they attacked her faith and her pious practices, it was that they might emancipate her from groundless prejudices and a servile bondage, and raise her to the level of the time. The Vicomte de la Rochefoucauld, in particular, set his heart on undoing the education of his daughter-in-law—according to him, it was quite out of date. He soon found that he would be obliged to renounce this project; but, while he resigned himself, because he could not help it, to seeing an image of the Middle Ages seated at his fireside, he at least entertained no apprehension that any other person in his house would be infected by retrograde ideas. How mistaken were the views of the sceptical philosopher! The influence of the Christian woman began to make itself felt. How could such mingled strength and sweetness, such patient firmness, united to such true and gentle goodness, be resisted? In all the actions of the young Duchess there was exquisite delicacy and tact, in all her sentiments there was true nobility; her relations with every one in the house were easy and pleasant. Facts like these were in themselves convincing; no one cognisant of them could deny that in the heart of the young and fervent Christian were stored up rich treasures of tenderness, devotedness, and fidelity. The Vicomtesse de la Rochefoucauld was the first to yield to the invincible power of goodness; she loved her daughter-in-law better than her own children. Madame de Durtal, the elder sister of the Duc de Doudeauville, was also deeply attached to her. This lady was clever, charming, and accomplished, but her natural qualities lacked the solid basis of faith and the sweet savour of piety. Hereafter we shall learn how she was led back to God by her sister-in-law's holy example.

It was, however, only by slow degrees that Madame de Doudeauville extended and fixed her gentle rule. Ere she had won the souls which were so dear to her, her own soul had to pass through many searching trials, and she was suffering from complete isolation in the midst of family life when the approaching arrival of her husband was announced to her. The news filled her with hope; she had the utmost need of affection, sincere, simple, true, constant, and lawful. Was such an affection to be granted to her need and to her prayers?

She began to dream of happiness after the image she found in her own heart: happiness in the conformity of views and feelings, in reciprocal esteem, in close union in well doing, in the unreserved sharing of all joys and all sorrows. She had much to give; what should she receive in return? Her young husband's letters led her to hope that he had been kept from evil ways, that his life was pure and pious; and yet, what were his surroundings and associates? He had recently made an excursion in Italy with his father: had not that changed the course and current of his ideas? All these thoughts strove in the mind of the young Duchess, and filled her with solicitude. She strove to conceal every sentiment except joyful anticipation, and she prayed without ceasing.

The expected day came, and the carriage wheels were heard in the court-yard of the château. Every one went down to welcome the travellers, the anxious, almost frightened young wife came last. The travelling-carriage drew up, and the door was opened, but the Duke, unutterably confused and bewildered, looked about him without seeing anything, and sat motionless in his place. A significant push from his father recalled him to his senses, he jumped out, flung his arms around the first person he encountered, and exclaimed: "My dear wife, what happiness to see you again!" while he pressed to his bosom an old house steward of sixty. A little behind the pair stood the Duchess, pale, and astonished at the mistake, which, however ludicrous, was very gracefully repaired. When the inevitable awkwardness of the meeting had passed away, the mutual impressions of the young pair were exceedingly favourable, and their married life commenced under happy auspices. The Vicomte de la Rochefoucauld soon began to suspect that the notions which had been at first entertained respecting his son's wife were unfounded, and went on to discover that she was as intelligent as she was good. The young couple, who found in each other all that they had respectively hoped for, enjoyed for some years wedded happiness as sacred and complete as this world could afford.

The privacy which they prized so highly, was too frequently interrupted by the obligation, which the rank of the Duke and Duchess imposed upon them, of appearing at the brilliant court festivals which enlivened the early years of the reign of Louis the Sixteenth. A succession of entertainments filled the royal residences by turns with light and movement, now the Tuileries, again Versailles, anon Trianon or Marly, was the scene of balls, theatrical representations, concerts, hunting parties, and every conceivable kind of amusement. The thorns which lurked beneath the flowers that decked the gay and heedless life of the great at that epoch were soon to pierce the feet which trod upon them; already calumny and evil-speaking mingled with the laughter of the gay and frivolous throng, who were dancing on the verge of an abyss. The young Duchesse de Doudeauville, who stood high in the favour of the Queen and the Princesses, and especially in that of Madame Elizabeth, the King's sister, passed on her way in the midst of all this frivolous life, gentle, serene, and blameless. The admiration of which she was the object had no intoxicating charm for her. The youth and inexperience of the Duke and Duchess invested them with peculiar interest, and the remarkable beauty of the wife more than sufficed to atone to society for the occasional mistakes of the husband, which were due to his excessive shyness, and to which he alludes, in his Memoirs, with a pleasant frankness. Among the anecdotes of those early halcyon days, we find one which claims a place here, so fitly does it illustrate the character of the Duke, and the impression created by the Duchess upon the fools and fribbles of the day.

On a certain occasion the Duc de Doudeauville, dining with the Prince de Condé, was seated beside one of those presumptuous bores, never wanting in society, who pronounce voluble and unhesitating opinions upon every variety of subject, and are especially distinguished by a spirit of opposition. This young man, after dealing out his judgments upon people and things with perfect self-complacency, mentioned the name of the Duchesse de Doudeauville, without the slightest suspicion that he was addressing her husband. The Duke made no remark. The young coxcomb continued :—

"Everybody talks about her charms, but she does not possess the talent of pleasing me."

Then he went on to detail the reasons, to which explanation his auditor, still keeping silence, and without betraying any surprise, listened with a smile, until one of the Prince's guests, seated at the opposite side of the table, addressed the Duc de Doudeauville by name. The unhappy critic of the Duchess was overwhelmed with confusion; he reddened, he stammered, he tried to unsay his former assertions, but the Duke stopped him, saying mildly:—"Calm yourself, my good friend, calm yourself, I beg. All that is essential for a woman like Madame de Doudeauville is that she shall please her husband. Make your mind easy, your opinion will not change mine, which is, that my wife is all she ought to be, in every respect."

It is pleasant to dwell upon the new-found, full, and sacred happiness of this epoch in the saintly life which we are contemplating. The more we see of that life, the more strongly it will prove to us that faith, religion rightly understood, enlightened piety, form a strict alliance in the heart wherein they reign with those tender and lawful affections which they sanctify, and so render eternal.

Madame de Doudeauville was deeply attached to her sister, Madame de Montesquiou. As children they had consoled each other under the strange and harsh treatment they endured at the hands of their mother. After their respective marriages, the sisters continued to meet as often as possible, and they sustained each other in the performance of their respective duties, in the midst of innumerable difficulties. Their mutual affection was never obscured by the lightest cloud. When, on the reading of the will of the Marquis de Cortenvaux, their grandfather, it was found that its dispositions were more largely in favour of Madame de Montesquiou than of her sister, Madame de Doudeauville warmly embraced the favoured heiress, exclaiming, "How glad I am!" She rejoiced in this disposition of their grandfather's property, which did away, to some extent, with the great disproportion between the fortunes of the two sisters.

The death of the Marquis de Cortenvaux, which occurred in July 1781, placed the Duchess in possession of the estate of Montmirail, in Marne, the scene of the last battle of 1814. Her father had borne the title, as next heir, but he had never owned the lands. On the occasion of her going thither to take possession of her patrimony, great rejoicings took place throughout the district. The Duchess acknowledged the homage which was paid her with exquisite grace and simplicity, and returned it by noble generosity to the poor. She was a true Lady Bountiful, a " châtelaine" such as the most brilliant fancies of the poets might have pictured.

The Duc de Doudeauville, faithful to the ancient traditions of his house, had entered the army, and was, in consequence, frequently obliged to leave his family for periods of uncertain duration. He greatly regretted those enforced absences, and took advantage of every free hour to return to the wife whom he loved and esteemed more and more each day of his life, and whose advice and example became urgently needful to counterbalance the perfidious influence of dangerous friends. He was invulnerable as regarded the principles of religion, but he was on the point of abandoning its practices, from excess of scrupulosity to which he was peculiarly susceptible, as his self-distrusting disposition inclined towards spiritual fear. His position obliged him to take part in the entertainments and amusements of the court; then how should he dare to approach the sacraments under such circumstances, living in so worldly a sphere? —to do so was to fail in respect for holy things. These considerations, which were constantly pressed upon him, profoundly affected the mind of the Duke, and he was actually about to deprive himself of his Easter Communion, when an unreserved conversation with his wife revealed the snare which had been set for him. The Duchess perfectly succeeded in convincing him of the difference between an obligation attached to his position, and an inclination of his own.

She who thus watched over the soul of

her husband had yet another mission to fulfil. The wise and faithful wife was destined to become, in still greater perfection, a model for mothers.

CHAPTER III.

THE SERVANT OF GOD IN HER HOME-LIFE.

AMONG the family portraits of the house of De la Rochefoucauld, those which recall the features of her who was at once a mother and a saint are cherished with a truly filial love. On one of these we gaze with peculiar pleasure and special reverence; it is not that of the Duchess in her venerable old age; nor that of the brilliant young beauty whom the crowd received with acclamations; it is that of the young mother, radiant with happiness, and holding her infant treasure in her arms. Her face wears its habitual expression of angelic sweetness, but the new love, joy, and tenderness lend it a fresh bloom and an additional charm. The bud which nestles beside the flower completes the lovely picture; the little Ernestine sleeps, smiling, on her fair young mother's bosom.

Happy was the child who found such a shelter. She was endowed with all the riches of heaven and of earth. The mother who held her in her arms with joy unspeakable, who watched with solicitude over her cradle, was not solely engaged in warding off every danger from the fragile little life; she was also seeking the Divine breath which had been breathed into the human creature whom Almighty God had committed to her keeping, and respect was mingled with her maternal love.

The constant care of the Duchesse de Doudeauville was to preserve intact the innocence of her child, to ward off the approach of evil, to fill her heart with faith and love; this sublime aim occupied her thoughts and inspired all her actions. She was well aware that first impressions, even though received before the age of reason, are vital and durable in a child's mind; and so she was careful that none but good examples should be presented to the observation of her little daughter, and she observed similar precautions in the case of her son, who was born two years later than Ernestine. On the occasions when she was absolutely obliged to relinquish her children to the temporary charge of others, she carefully selected such persons for the trust as would unite with her in mind and principles, and aid her to develop the intelligence of the little girl and boy by means of sound and solid truth. No ridiculous fables, no silly rhymes and stories, were offered to the lively and ardent imagination of Ernestine and Sosthenes, but yet they had their share in the marvellous, in that for which we all yearn from our cradles, because the secret instinct which tells us of the grandeur of our future destiny also impels us to seek that greatness beyond the visible horizon of our lives.

While she withheld from her children the vain chimeras with which the infant mind is generally amused, this loving and faithful mother, without departing from the real, transported them to the heavenly land. She told them of their eternal country, she painted its beauties, she showed them the prepared place and the promised crown. She spoke to her children of the holy angels and the Blessed Virgin, she made them visible to their minds' eye ; she presented to them the Infant Jesus, their Divine example, and the children kissed the hands and feet of the image of the holy child with reverent love. Then came the history of the saints and the martyrs; and as nature ever desires a contrast, instead of monsters and phantoms, the Duchess showed her children the abyss of perdition, side by side with the heavenly city, and, lurking behind their guardian angels, the enemy who goeth about ceaselessly, seeking whom he may devour. She inspired her children with her own sentiments, thus giving them a second life derived from herself. All that she loved they loved, with all that she thought beautiful they were enraptured; if she were sad their tears flowed; her influence over them was unbounded. Madame de Doudeauville was profoundly sensible of the great responsibility which such an influence laid upon her; she strove more and more ardently after Christian perfection: one might have said of her that she held in her hands the entire future fate of her children.

The Duchess earnestly desired that her son and daughter should retain their simplicity and childish frankness; and she never permitted them to be foolishly flattered and petted, either by strangers or by members of the family and household. She did not allow their sayings and doings to be repeated in their presence, and she trained them to be gracious and courteous to all; to return thanks for every service rendered to them, to give alms with generous grace, and taught them to deny themselves a passing gratification in order that they might have more to give. Their greatest reward was to be taken to visit the poor, and to offer them with their own hands the fruits of their little acts of self-denial. She especially feared that her children might be tempted into vanity and self-indulgence, the ordinary consequences of wealth and luxury, and she therefore strove to counteract the dangerous effects of their rank and fortune by her lessons and by her own example, teaching them the necessity for self-restraint, and, crucifix in hand, gently explaining to them the merit of suffering. Thus did she ensure the future happiness of her children much more effectually than those blindly fond mothers who heap every possible indulgence upon their children, under the pretext that it is well to allow them to enjoy life as much as they can during its earliest years. Mothers such as these, who will not suffer their children to be opposed in anything, leave them undefended against the inevitable trials of life, and incapable of carrying its burthens. A truly wise mother will let her child see the thorn, though she saves him from the scratch. She will show him the difficulty, aid and encourage him to surmount it, and teach him to appreciate the merit and the happiness of self-conquest. Thus will she prepare him for the strife, from which it is not in her power to shelter him; thus gird him for the battle which is the common lot.

The grand and inspiriting narratives of the Old and New Testament formed admirable texts for the lessons of Madame de Doudeauville. An ineffaceable impression was made on the minds and hearts of the children by the striking pictures of vice and virtue, of reward and chastisement, contained in the Holy Scriptures, and they took an inexhaustible interest in that union of the marvellous with the true, of startling miracle with the bold simplicity of the earliest ages of the world, which forms one of the most powerful charms of the Biblical record.

To their mother the children carried all their little confidences, their joys and griefs, their wishes or their fears; each and all alike found room in that heart, so indulgent, and yet so free from weakness. Every fault was fully and readily acknowledged to her, who so faithfully trained the consciences of her children. So gentle and so patient was their mother with them, that the brother and sister never thought of seeking any other friend. This filial confidence became the safeguard of Ernestine, whose happy lot it was to remain under her mother's protection until her marriage. Her brother was less fortunate; the vicissitudes of the Revolution forced Madame de Doudeauville to submit to separation from her son on several occasions.

While the Duchess was thus fulfilling her maternal duties, she was also pursuing her apostolic mission to her husband's family—a mission none the less active because it was silent; her soul, displayed before the eyes of God, was full of zeal, but her perfect tact led her to await the moment of grace in patience. Madame de la Rochefoucauld was the first to yield to the influence of her daughter-in-law. She began by admiring her, then she advanced to the desire and purpose of imitating her; and she finally associated herself with her in all her good works with hearty sincerity.

Another person also was brought under this benign influence, but she concealed her surrender for a long time. This was the Comtesse de Durtal, who was divided between the power of old prejudices and the charm of the Christian life always before her eyes. The young Duchess little suspected the strife which she had kindled, and which raged long in the heart of her sister-in-law. In later days she spoke of Madame de Durtal as follows :—

"I loved my sister-in-law very much, and was much beloved by her. I prayed constantly for her; and when we were together, and I observed how cleverly she would turn off the irreligious and back-biting talk which was so painful to me, I was deeply touched. I wished very much to let her see how grateful I felt, and to speak to her of God, but I was always stopped by the fear of not being able to cope with her objections and arguments. I felt sure that a conversion of this kind must come from the inward touch of grace, rather than from any success in controversy; but yet that conviction did not hinder me from writing long letters to her when I was alone, letters in which I refuted, one by one, the errors to which I had heard her give utterance. I was stronger with my pen than I should have been in conversation, but before I had laid any of my documents before her, she came to my room one morning, at five o'clock, in tears, threw herself into my arms, and said:

"'I cannot bear this any longer. I have not closed my eyes all night. You preach to me in everything except words; why is it that you will never speak to me of God?'

"I led her to my writing-table, and took from a drawer the voluminous manuscript which had occupied me for so long.

"'Read this,' I said, 'and judge whether I think of you.'"

The ice was broken; long conversations between the sisters-in-law ensued; and when, a few days afterwards, Madame de Doudeauville went away to Luchon, she had not to suffer long from suspense about her beloved convert. Shortly after her arrival, she received a joyful letter from her mother-in-law, announcing that the Comtesse de Durtal had gone to Confession and received Holy Communion. Madame de Montagu was present when this good news arrived, and she saw the Duchess change countenance and burst into tears.

"What is the matter?" asked Madame de Montagu, taking her friend's hand.

Madame de Doudeauville informed her of the source of her joyful tears, and the two friends straightway repaired to the little neighbouring church to offer their thanksgiving to Almighty God. This was indeed a glorious victory; for Madame de Durtal, a woman of strong mind and generous nature, threw herself with fervour into the practices of piety, and became a shining example of Christian virtues. Her conversion preceded by five years her truly heroic death.

It was more difficult to win over the

Vicomte de la Rochefoucauld, although he had been brought to render full justice to his daughter-in-law, and was now full of kindness and consideration for her. The change in his feelings towards her even extended to his reposing especial confidence in her, to which the Duchess responded by care and kindness, and by certain attentions prompted by the delicacy of her perceptions and by her keen sympathy. So well did she behave to him, that at length the Vicomte began to take positive pleasure, and to discern an actual charm, in her society. This happy and welcome transformation (for it was nothing less) was followed by a result which the young Duchess most ardently desired, but which the rooted scepticism of M. de la Rochefoucauld hardly permitted her to hope for. He was taken suddenly and seriously ill, dangerous symptoms declared themselves, and the progress of the disease was so rapid that the Duc de Doudeauville, who was absent, had barely time to reach Paris before the end came. The angel of the family was, however, watching by the dying man, and praying that the father might be with his children to all eternity. Thanks to her prayers and her efforts, the Vicomte received the last sacraments with full consciousness, and gave abundant proof of faith and repentance. Just before he died, he turned to his daughter-in-law and said, with emotion:

"I hope, my dear child, you are satisfied with me."

In her grief, the Duchess had a great consolation : God, by giving her this soul, amply recompensed her for all she had suffered for the faith since she had entered the family of the Vicomte. She deeply regretted her father-in-law, whose goodness of heart and loyal nature she had fully recognised through all his errors and delusions; but she repressed her own feelings, and occupied herself entirely in supporting and consoling her husband, whose grief was so great that for twenty-four hours after his father's death he was quite bewildered, and incapable of thought or action.

The death of the Vicomte de la Rochefoucauld, which occurred in 1789, involved the young couple in a great deal of trouble, and in an inheritance of debt and difficulty, owing to the maladministration of a man of business in whom the Vicomte had placed absolute confidence. This person had also had charge of Madame de Doudeauville's property for the first year after her marriage, and had brought about a deficit of one hundred thousand francs in a few months. The Duke and Duchess, who were very justly alarmed by this, took a step which evinced a degree of determination not common at seventeen years of age.

They made up their minds that remonstrance would be useless, and that amendment was impossible, and they forthwith placed the administration of their property in the hands of a person selected by themselves. Their choice was fortunate; the new agent found means to repair the breach made in their fortune without touching their capital. With equal skill he regulated the affairs of the deceased Vicomte de la Rochefoucauld. In all matters of the kind the Duchess had remarkably sound judgment and great decision; her natural kindness and gentleness did not prevent her from adhering firmly to any resolution founded upon right and justice.

· · · · ·

The year '89 began. The tempest was gathering fast, and men's hearts were beginning to fail them for fear. A few attempted to make light of the political and social condition of France at that threatening epoch, but the Duc de Doudeauville was not of their number. He was profoundly affected, and seriously apprehensive; he distinctly foresaw the fatal issue to which the popular movement was tending, and it most fortunately occurred to him to effect a division between his own property and that of his wife. His relatives and friends vainly endeavoured to dissuade him from a design in which they could discern no advantage for him. It was folly, in their eyes, to hand over an income of more than a hundred and twenty thousand livres to the absolute control of a woman of twenty-five. The Duke, who was entirely unconvinced by their remonstrances, persisted in his project, and, as it afterwards proved, saved his children from the forfeiture of their fortune by doing so. He well knew that he might depend with absolute confidence upon the wife and mother to whom he confided this onerous charge.

As "bailli" of Chartres, it was the Duke's duty to preside over an assembly of between five and six hundred persons who were to elect the deputies to the States General. A numerous faction wanted to set aside his presidency, as a protestation against nomination by the King; but his firmness and calmness overcame their opposition. Great, however, was his embarrassment when, after the opening speech, the majority demanded the vote by individuals, and not by "order," this being contrary to the instructions which had been received. The Duc de Doudeauville then adopted an ingenious method of solving the difficulty, one which enabled him to do his duty faithfully, and yet without exciting either murmuring or opposition. "Before we commence our deliberations," said he, "we must verify our powers, and we must divide in order to save time in that business. The several names are proposed." Having then invited the nobles to accompany him, and begged the bishop to place himself at the head of his clergy, he rose, and each man present followed his president. The orders being thus separated, the Duke took care they did not again get mixed. Notwithstanding this manœuvre, the entire meeting passed a vote of thanks to the Duke, who, not having attained the prescribed age, was not qualified for a place in the Constituent Assembly. He was therefore obliged to remain a mute spectator of the insensate scenes which formed the prelude to the most terrible and sanguinary catastrophe which history records. Finding himself absolutely powerless to offer any obstacle to the revolutionary tide, he decided on travelling in Italy for a while with all his family.

In passing through Nice, the Duke tried to cross the Var by a ford, an act of imprudence which exposed him to considerable danger. He tells the story of this adventure as follows:—

"The river had been impassable for several days, the rains had swollen it to the proportions of a torrent a kilometer in width; and our six horses came to a dead stop, unable to cope with the strength and swiftness of the stream. The water was invading the carriage; all the efforts of the postilions and of our guides were useless, and the danger was increasing every moment, when I espied six post-horses in the distance, coming along the coast-road from Nice. I managed to get myself carried somehow between two of the men (on the shoulders of one, and held on by the other) to the river-bank, and went in search of this unlooked-for help. The men in charge of the post-horses required a great deal of persuasion to induce them to help us, and only yielded at last when I held up a handful of louis, and promised that they should have them all. It was with great difficulty that the men and horses reached the carriage. Then came another scene of bargaining with my bearers, to induce them to carry me back to the place of danger. My wife and children were there, and I was determined to save them or to perish with them. By the help of God, and after long and exhausting efforts, we were at last taken out of the river. In a short time we arrived at Nice, and from thence we went on to Genoa."

The foreign noble enjoyed sundry rights at Genoa in consideration of his being a grandee of Spain. In fact, he ranked with the Doge, and, among other privileges, had only to mention his title in order to have the chains, which prevented the circulation of vehicles in almost all the streets, taken down before his carriage. For him the city gates were opened after the regulation hours, and he employed that privilege to enable him to pass his evenings at the neighbouring country-houses, at which the greater number of the Genoese nobility resided during the summer. Many were the important personages, residents in the city, senators and others, who used to solicit permission to accompany the young "emigré," so as to extend their absence beyond the regulation limit.

The Duke and Duchess passed several months in Italy, and their sojourn was marked by an incident which Madame de Doudeauville, with characteristic discretion, concealed from every one. Her husband, however, has revealed it in order to do homage to her merits, which were indeed of a kind and degree of which the world seldom sees an example. A life of pleasure, in a land of enchantment, was not without its dangers for a man of twenty-five, full of spirits and activity, and of a sensitive and impressionable disposition. He had no serious occupation, and he naturally amused himself in the society of agreeable people. One of these was a beautiful Italian lady, and the idle hours which he passed with her were so seductive, that his imagination was completely captivated. A little more, and his heart might have been won also.

What were the feelings of the saintly Duchess at this time ? She never made any allusion to the secret pain which the change in her husband, of which she was perfectly well aware, occasioned her; she never spoke of the matter at all; but she afterwards referred to this particular epoch in her life in the following terms :—

"The world," she said, "had overturned

G

all the ideas which I had formed of the simple and natural relations of man with God. I was utterly saddened by the perversity and error which I saw around me. It seemed to me that I was a participator in this impiety, and I no longer dared to approach the holy table. Once, my fear so completely overcame me, that I very nearly fainted in church. I was tormented by scruples which I could neither analyse for myself nor explain to my Confessor. I consulted a Jesuit, a very clever and experienced man, who never entered into discussions. He cured me by making me perform an Act of Obedience, which I can never remember without emotion. I was at Genoa, and so unhappy about myself, and the turmoil within me, that, not satisfied with going to Confession on the day before my Communions, I used to return in the morning, though I had to go a long distance, and even then I frequently could not make up my mind to go up to the altar rails. One day I presented myself in this way, to receive a fresh absolution, and my Confessor, instead of listening to me, addressed me.

"'Are you fasting?' he asked.

"'Yes, father.'

"'Go to the altar rail then, and I will come and give you Communion.'

"I obeyed him, tremblingly, and from that moment my fears ceased."

It is most likely that the trouble in the heart of the Duchess contributed to this painful spiritual condition, and augmented it. However that may be, trusting in the Divine protection, she preserved her customary manner towards her husband totally unchanged. She treated him with unvarying sweetness, tenderness, and respect, and if a shade of sadness passed over her countenance, the tacit reproach had no anger in it. The Duke would, no doubt, have been aroused to a sense of the suffering he was inflicting upon her, had not the fascination of the moment thrown over his danger, as it always does, that reassuring illusion, "I will go no farther."

Madame de Doudeauville had too much judgment to be in any doubt as to the only remedy for this dangerous state of things. She would not indeed impose it, but she proposed it, with her usual tact and gracefulness. One day she received a letter from her sister, Madame de Montesquiou, announcing her intention of quitting France, and the Duchess took advantage of this opportunity to express a wish to join her. The Duke, although he was greatly agitated by the proposal, did not refuse to accede to it, and the risk of missing the traveller rendered it necessary that their departure for Annécy should be immediate. But he carried a perturbed heart with him, and sad, weary, and gloomy, he went about among the majestic mountains of Switzerland, a distressful spectacle of utter ennui. Then his wife, perfectly aware of the cause of his melancholy, and having up to that time kept a dignified and discreet silence, addressed him with the greatest serenity :—

"You are in trouble; I know it, I see it; why do you not tell me about it. Let me share your grief, and perhaps I may diminish it."

The Duke, deeply touched by this advance on his wife's part, responded to it by a complete disclosure. He concealed nothing from her, and the weight at his heart was lightened. "This avowal," he says, "solicited with so much grace, and received with so much indulgence, did me good. My mind became more calm, and I abandoned my intention of returning to Genoa." She who could lay her hand upon such waves to still them, must have had her soul's dwelling above the earth. Madame de Doudeauville, in the eyes of her husband and her friends, was placed in an upper sphere, which human passions could not reach.

The exiles resided at Annécy for fifteen months, and their sojourn was a period not only of enjoyment but of spiritual refreshment. The country abounded in memorials of Saint François de Sales; throughout the district and its environs living testimonies to his ardent charity were to be found, and produced a deep impression upon the Duc de Doudeauville. He needed a season of serious and solitary reflection, to which the actual condition of things conduced; the state of France, the extreme gravity of passing events, the vicissitudes of human affairs, the doom of " passing away " written upon all things, and which he began to feel and to understand; all combined to teach him to appreciate the wisdom and the happiness of one who had devoted his life to the salvation of souls. While praying upon the tomb of the Saint, he felt a strong desire to make a solemn affirmation of his faith. Hitherto his natural shyness had rendered him accessible to the persuasions of human respect; but he now made a firm resolution that he would make himself known everywhere, and always, as a practical and faithful Catholic. The Duchess thanked God devoutly for the sensible progress of her husband in the spiritual life, and for her own part enjoyed to the utmost the peace and retirement, which were particularly delightful after the gaiety and the stir of life at Genoa. Her soul had come out of a severe trial strengthened and happy, and she would not if she could have obliterated from her life that which she had suffered by the grace of God. Do not we also feel, as we follow the phases of a life as admirable as it is lovely, and as we contemplate the extent of the sacrifices which it reveals, that we would not erase those pages from the noble and touching story, which exhibit the brightness of the believer's triumph, while they reveal the depths of her suffering?

The Duke and Duchess became acquainted with the De Sales family, who had inherited something of the piety and amiability of the saintly bishop. Frequent visits were interchanged, to the mutual satisfaction of the two families; for it was not long before the merits of Madame de Doudeauville were recognised by her new friends. In Savoy she also made the acquaintance of the Abbé de Thiollaz, to whom she subsequently rendered an all-important service during the French Revolution. This worthy ecclesiastic, perceiving that the Duchess was strongly attracted towards the poor and all holy persons, mentioned a very pitiable case to her. It was that of a poor woman, who suffered from severe bodily ailments, but on whom Almighty God bestowed much sensible favour. After her Communions, when she believed herself to be quite alone in the church, the poor creature would make her thanksgiving aloud, in a most affecting manner, and utter, doubtless under the inspiration of the Holy Spirit, truly admirable thoughts and supplications. Madame de Doudeauville expressed a wish to visit this afflicted servant of our Divine Lord, and on seeing her she was shocked at the condition in which she found her. The poor creature could only drag herself along on her hands and knees, and her nails had grown unnaturally long and rugged. Madame de Doudeauville begged to be allowed to cut these revolting nails; and the poor suffering woman, looking attentively at the beautiful and elegant lady who was thus touched with compassion for her, stretched out one hand as though she would accept the proffered service. The Duchess took out her scissors, but the poor woman quickly withdrew her hand from that of her visitor, and said, with much significance: "That is enough, you do not despise the poor, the members of Jesus Christ."

On her return to France, in later days, Madame de Doudeauville learned with thankfulness, from the Abbé de Thiollaz, that this holy woman had prayed for her shortly before her death.

Her brief halt at Annécy, in the journey of life, the repose which she gained in prayer and in tranquil contemplation of the beauties of nature, served as a preparation for the great struggle which awaited the Duchess, and all the nobility of France. The signal for the strife had already been given from all quarters of the doomed kingdom.

At the commencement of 1792, the Duc de Doudeauville set out for Paris, where he had important business to arrange, and whither he determined to go in order that he might ascertain for himself what was the real condition of the public mind. His wife, who was extremely anxious to follow him, had entreated him to question his friends as to the feasibility of her doing so; and his report of their opinions being generally favourable, she also returned to her native country. The re-union of the husband and father with his wife and children was, however, but of brief duration. The Duc de Doudeauville, in spite of his repugnance to the emigration movement among the aristocracy, was induced by the hope of saving his King, and delivering his country from an odious tyranny, to part from all who were most dear to him. With an aching heart he bade them adieu, and set out for the banks of the Rhine, to place his sword at the service of that cause with which he fondly believed the salvation of his country to be identified. One short and disastrous campaign convinced him that the coalition hid ambitious designs of its own under the avowed project of delivering the King and restoring order in France; and then, despairing of any good result, he quitted the army, and condemned himself to long and painful inaction.

CHAPTER IV.

DURING THE REVOLUTION.

THE Duchesse de Doudeauville, who had remained insensible to the blandishments of a splendid court life, and had been humble, calm, and consequently strong, in the days of her prosperity, was not dismayed when she was called upon to confront the perils of the Revolution. The events which brought her face to face with difficulty and danger of various kinds will but show us more clearly what treasures of heroic charity and courage are stored up in a heart wherein God has established His reign. We shall see her faithful to her mission, invariably prudent, but still more remarkable for devotedness, forgetful of herself in her solicitude for those who depended on her; succouring the unfortunate, and defending the interests of religion, wherever her voice or her influence could reach.

While she continued at liberty she was to be found by the bedside of the sick, at the prison-gates, seeking for priests and leading them to the dying, saving the Holy Eucharist from profanation, even at the peril of her own life. On one occasion a priest, who was in momentary fear of being arrested, hastily placed in her hands the sacred box from which he had just taken the Host to be administered to a dying man. She carried away the temporary Tabernacle, in which a consecrated particle remained, with the deepest respect, and placed it in her *prie Dieu*, which already contained a Host. This it was her inestimable privilege to possess, so that, if in imminent danger of death, she might administer the Holy Communion to herself. Notwithstanding the danger of the time, and the rigorous inquisition which had been established, the Duchess contrived to have Mass said almost every day in her house.

At the Convent of the Visitation, in the Rue du Bac, the chaplain had been imprisoned, and seals placed upon the Tabernacle, to await the arrival of a priest who had taken the oath to the Revolutionary Government.* The Duchess, deeply afflicted at the idea of such a profanation, proposed to the Superior that she should be permitted to carry off the Sacred Hosts reserved in the Tabernacle, at her own sole risk and peril; but the Superior, while she praised the zeal of the Duchess, refused the permission for which she begged,

* "Prêtres assermentés" is the phrase by which these unhappy men were described.—*Translator.*

saying that she could not accept the responsibility of compromising the Duchess, and all the community, however willing she might be to expose herself personally to danger.

Notwithstanding that the penalty of death had been pronounced against all who should shelter those priests who remained faithful to their vows, the Duchess gave refuge in her house to the Abbé Vinclimput, a German ecclesiastic; and with delicacy equal to her generosity, she was most anxious that he should not discover at what risk to her he was enjoying her hospitality. It was inevitable that one of the servants should be in the secret, and this man, alarmed on his mistress' account, and also on his own, informed the good priest, who immediately declared that nothing should induce him to expose the kind family, to whom he already owed so much, to so terrible a danger.

In vain the Duchess implored him to stay with her; he persisted in leaving the shelter of her roof, was arrested on the following day, and immediately executed.

Madame de Doudeauville was too important a personage to be forgotten or overlooked by the leaders of the Revolution. On the 28th May 1793, while she was present at Mass with her mother-in-law and Madame de Durtal, she was warned that a crowd of *bonnets rouges* had just swarmed in at the gateway of the hôtel. She instantly rose from her knees, went in search of the intruders, and having induced them to go into the garden, she diverted their attention until she knew that the Holy Sacrifice was terminated. When she was satisfied that the priest had had time to escape, she re-entered the house with her ruffianly visitors, who immediately arrested her, as well as Madame de la Rochefoucauld and the Comtesse de Durtal. She was taken to the Rue de Sévres, and lodged in a house which, until the previous day, had been used as a barrack. On the threshhold of this dismal dwelling, the little Ernestine, then hardly eleven years old, clung round her mother's neck, and refused to leave her. The child was torn from her mother's arms, whose bitter tears and supplications failed to procure her permission to see her from whom she had never previously been absent for a single day. The agony of the child wrung the heart of the mother, but it did not shake her courage; that was not to be assailed by any human means. Madame de Doudeauville gave her daughter her solemn blessing, and spoke to her with cheerful confidence, even in the dreadful moment of parting. Then, repressing her own grief, she applied herself to calm and cheer her companions. The three ladies were locked up in a bare and dilapidated room, whose entire furniture consisted of three old mattresses. The Duchess placed one of these above another, so as to make a comfortable seat for her mother and sister-in-law, and lavished upon them every possible care and attention.

Madame de Doudeauville, who occupied herself solely in endeavouring to alleviate the imprisonment of her mother and sister-in-law, obtained several indulgences for them; and so much did her courage, serenity, and goodness impress the gaolers, that when the noble prisoners were restored to liberty after only eight days' detention, they greeted the warrant with applause.

Only for a short time, however, did Ernestine de la Rochefoucauld enjoy the happiness of being restored to her mother. The three ladies were arrested a second time, and subjected to a term of imprisonment which, though less rigorous, lasted longer than the former. For two whole months they were forced to endure constant visits from the Revolutionary authorities, to submit to being searched, and questioned at all hours, and to hearing denunciations and threats of death directed against them. All through this trying ordeal the character of Madame de Doudeauville shone with added brilliance; she was as dignified and as firm as she was gentle and patient; she commanded both admiration and respect. One night, when she had thrown a little water out of her window, she heard a great noise outside her room; the gaolers were alarmed. "What is that extraordinary noise?" said they; "no doubt the prisoner has contrived to convey a letter to her co-conspirators." It really seemed as if the country were in danger. The gaolers knocked loudly, and the Duchess rose, opened the door, and replied quietly:

"Go and see for yourselves, my friends." They retired, disconcerted by her unconcern, and allowed her to sleep in peace.

At length she was liberated, and she immediately occupied herself with her children, and in assisting a great number of poor and otherwise unhappy persons. She hoped now to have had a little breathing time in which to enjoy the society of her mother and sister-in-law, with whom she was in every respect in perfect harmony, but no such respite in the fiery trial of her life at this terrible epoch was accorded to her. Three days after their liberation, the Vicomtesse de la Rochefoucauld and the Comtesse de Durtal were arrested for the third time. On this occasion they were immured with some English nuns, who were themselves prisoners in their own convent. Madame de Doudeauville was saved from sharing their fate by a line of conduct on her own part which would have seemed certain to lead to her destruction. She had to undergo a strict and lengthened interrogatory concerning her husband, and she replied with absolute frankness and loyalty to every question. Her questioner launched into invectives against the "*emigré;*" and she answered by a warm defence of him, notwithstanding the reiterated signs which the Vicomtesse, who was terrified by her boldness, made to her.

"You are then really afflicted by his absence?" she was asked.

"Yes, certainly I am."

"You regret him then?"

"Much."

"Well, citizeness, I see you are a good woman; you shall come to no harm."

And, in fact, on the following day, when the Section heard the report of the examination of the Duchess, they unanimously applauded her dauntless truth.

The claims of her duty as daughter, sister, and mother, and her strong desire to fulfil them perfectly, suggested to the Duchess to place herself and her daughter Ernestine as boarders in the convent where her relatives were detained. The Superior received her joyfully, but she and Ernestine were hardly installed in their new abode when a fresh and far more terrible misfortune fell upon the unhappy prisoners.

To the true Christian the hour of great sacrifices is also the hour of heroic virtues. If Nature, shuddering at the chalice, tries to push it away, and utters the same cry which escaped from the most compassionate love that ever filled a heart—"Take away this cup from me!"—Grace adds, after the example of the Divine Saviour, and in His strength, "Thy will, not mine be done." Blessed and happy is that believer who loses neither faith nor confidence in the time of trial.

On the 8th March 1794, the Comtesse de Durtal, being summoned to appear before the Revolutionary Tribunal, tore herself from her mother's arms, and went to receive the sentence of death, which she accepted calmly. On being taken to the Conciergerie, she found there her uncle, M. de l'Aigle, who had been the involuntary cause of her arrest, and in their meeting the hand of Providence was made manifest in a wonderful manner. While the Count was bitterly lamenting, not his own fate, but that of the young woman whom he had compromised by an insignificant letter which he had carelessly left on his writing-table, his niece, full of sublime courage and fervent piety, profited by the few hours of life which remained to them both, and acting like an apostle to the condemned man, she pleaded with him for his own soul. Her work received the benediction of God; she led back to Him a soul which had strayed from Him, and she was happy to purchase that privilege at the cost of her life. So grand and devout was her bearing to the last moment, that her very guards were softened, and prayed with her. One of them became converted, and afterwards affirmed that he had never witnessed so fearless and pious a death.

Madame de Doudeauville, who had vainly exhausted every effort to get into the Conciergerie, was much consoled by learning these details. She had lost a sister, a sweet and gentle companion, who, for the past five years had been rendered doubly dear by the conformity of their religious feelings; she keenly felt the grief of her mother-in-law, but so clear and present to her was the thought of the eternal reunion which awaited them, that her resignation was truly celestial. Very shortly afterwards farther intelligence reached her, which made her heart swell with mingled grief and pride. The Maréchal de Mouchy-Noailles, her uncle, had been executed, uttering as his last words this noble sentence, worthy of a hero and a martyr:

"At eighteen," he said, "I mounted to the assault for my King;* surely I well may, at eighty, mount the scaffold for my God!"

Events marched rapidly at that terrible time, and there was no pause or leisure in which friendship could pour the balm of consolation into the sufferer's wounds.

---

* The literal translation of this sentence reads awkwardly, but the force and simplicity of the grand saying of the Maréchal would be injured by any interference with it. —*Translator.*

Madame de Doudeauville was endeavouring to sustain Madame de la Rochefoucauld under the blow of her daughter's death; the afflicted woman at least hoped that they might be permitted to mourn together, when a decree was issued by the Convention, by which all the nobles who were not prisoners were ordered to leave Paris without delay. This was a fresh dagger-stroke to the unhappy women; the one had become, as it seemed, indispensable to the other; and yet, doubt or deliberation was out of the question. The Duchess had to think first of her husband and children, to whom she belonged; by remaining voluntarily in Paris she must risk a life which was not hers to give. The bereaved mother parted from her consoler with the deepest anguish of heart, indeed; but as Madame de Doudeauville lived always in the presence of the Divine Will, by which she interpreted every event, and accepted good and evil with equal submission, she had the power of inspiring those with whom she had any intercourse or dealings with something of the same cheerful obedience. She earnestly recommended her mother-in-law to the Superior of the community, and left the Vicomtesse wonderfully resigned, and hopeful of better days.

In order to quit Paris, it was necessary for the Duchess to procure permits for herself and her daughter, and nine witnesses were required. The Duchess, who knew no one in the neighbourhood of the convent, applied to the gardener, who, on the following day, brought her nine sponsors. On her arrival at the "Section," she found there a poor blind nun, who was the object of coarse mockery by the crowd. The Duchess accosted the frightened nun with graceful kindness, ascertained the nature of her business, and seeing that she was the bearer of a paper which required a signature, she led her to the official desk, and thus rescued her from the ridicule of the crowd. She was then turning patiently away to wait still longer on her own account, when a bystander, who had noticed her act of charity, said to the commissary in charge :—"I hope you will give a permit to the citizeness; she has been here three or four hours." She was then asked her quality. "Ex-noble," she replied. The questioner, who wanted to save her, was alarmed by her answer, and said quickly, in a low voice :—"Say rather, living on your own means." She understood, and replied as he had suggested, which in no way offended her conscience.

The president, who was struck by her

dignified frankness, took down her name and address, and gave her his own, begging her, if any need should arise, to apply to him. In narrating this incident long afterwards, she said simply:—"It was my youth and beauty which made him take an interest in me."

Madame de Doudeauville retired to the little village of Wissous, four leagues from Paris, and there continued to lead her truly apostolic life, while she closely watched over the education of her children. Several nuns of the Visitation, who had been driven out of their convent, were most hospitably received by her, and enjoyed seclusion and regularity almost equal to those of the cloister in her house. Madames de Barnage and de Noland took great pleasure in teaching Ernestine, and preparing her for her first Communion. When the dear child was twelve years old, her mother's room was transformed into a chapel, and there the greatest act of human life was accomplished, in a simple and affecting manner, in secrecy. Much caution was necessary in order to escape observation; but the pious Duchess had good and faithful servants, upon whom she might confidently rely.

During her sojourn at Wissous, it came to the knowledge of Madame de Doudeauville that a newly born infant in the village was in great danger of remaining unbaptized, because the child's parents were not acquainted with any faithful priest. She went immediately to the house, proposed her daughter Ernestine as godmother, and asked the mother to intrust her with the baby for a few minutes. When she had sprinkled her with the water of baptism, the Duchess kissed the new-made child of God with great tenderness, and restored her to her mother. Thenceforward she watched over her little protégée, to whom the kiss and the blessing of a saint were destined to bring good fortune. After the death of her daughter, the Duchess, whose chief aim in her own life was to do as much good as she could in the name of her beloved child, and for the sake of her dear memory, did not forget the godchild of Ernestine. The second Ernestine grew up to show herself unfailingly worthy of her benefactress, who had counted the happiness of this young girl, who was well educated and most prosperously married, and that of her family, among her greatest blessings. They owed all to her, and their gratitude was so sincere, and so warmly expressed, that the Duchess almost shrank from this earthly recompense.

While Wissous had only a priest who had taken the Revolutionary oath, Madame de Doudeauville never attended the parish church, but went to a distance of three leagues to hear mass, which was celebrated, in the strictest secrecy, at the house of Madame de Lucy, by M. de Bonnatier. But when the little village church was again blessed with the ministrations of a faithful pastor, the Duchess had it repaired, and furnished with the necessary ornaments and sacred vessels, so that the services might be fitly celebrated without delay.

To the Altar of God she had constant recourse for strength and consolation in the heaviest of the trials which she had to endure. She was uncertain, indeed almost completely ignorant, concerning her husband, and she often feared that he might be in want of the absolute necessaries of life. He had taken a quantity of plate and her diamonds with him, but she heard neither how much money the sale of these things had produced, nor

I

whether the funds thus raised were exhausted. Did the Duke know that his sister had been executed, and that his mother was in prison? No answers to the questions which rent her tender and troubled heart could reach her; she could only confide her pain to God, who reigned in that heart, and who, while He tried and chastened, had always marvellously protected her.

One day, just after the Duchess had made an act of confidence in God, she was told that a man, who had been sent by the Duke, requested an interview with her. This person was a confidential agent of the Duc de Doudeauville, and had been deputed by him to escort the Duchess and her children to the Duke's place of abode. All the necessary measures had been taken, that, by the aid of a disguise, the Duchess might pass for a relative of the agent, and be conducted in safety beyond the frontier. We may easily conceive with what eagerness the Duchess questioned this faithful servant concerning her beloved exile. What was he doing? How much did he know of the fate of those so dear to him? The Duke had not ventured to write to his wife; the danger to the messenger, if a letter had been found upon him, would have been too great. The agent was, however, able to tell her how great were the anxieties of the husband and father, how deep was the grief of the mourning brother. We learn from M. de Doudeauville himself in what manner he had learned the fact of his sister's death :—

"One day," he says, "when, according to my usual custom, I was reading aloud the English and French newspapers at a public reading-room, my hearers observed me suddenly turn pale, stagger, and speedily swoon away. I had caught sight of these lines in an article containing news from Paris: 'The citizeness Durtal and the citizen De l'Aigle were executed yesterday at the Place de la Révolution.' The horrible intelligence fell upon me like a thunderbolt. My sister, whom I loved so dearly! She was a widow, and, I said to myself, if they have killed her, will they not also kill the wife and the mother of the *emigré*? My existence was one of continuous suspense; I should rather say that I ceased to live, except in the sense of fear and pain. I waited for the post-days with agonising impatience, and when they dawned, they threw me into fits of dreadful anguish. I dreaded to find in each line of the newspaper the condemnation of some one who was dear to me. I know not how I, or any of those who had to endure them, lived through the anxieties of that time.

"A dear friend of Madame de Doudeauville, who was living at Brussels, having heard of the tragic event, and knowing how cruel and desolate my position was, set off with her husband in a country cart, which was the only vehicle their means enabled them to procure, and came to me. They brought me the only consolation which friendship can offer—prayers and tears."

This dear friend of Madame de Doudeauville was the Marquise de Montagu, a truly excellent and admirable woman, and who was to learn a few days later that her own mother, her grandmother, and her sister had been added to the list of the heroic victims of the Revolution.

After many days of intolerable suspense and apprehension, the Duc de Doudeauville intrusted to a native of Switzerland, in whom he had entire confidence, the onerous task of bringing his wife and children to him. The undertaking was to cost a large sum in proportion to the resources of the exile. An income of four thousand five hundred francs (one hundred and eighty pounds sterling) was all he had; and this he shared with the Marquise de Montmirail, who had taken refuge in England. No privations, however, could inflict so much suffering upon him as did the vision of the sword suspended over the dear ones whose safety he would gladly have purchased with his own life.

Madame de Doudeauville, who would have braved any danger for the sake of rejoining her husband, immediately set about her preparations; but, with her usual unfailing consideration, she made inquiries, before setting out, whether her departure could be used to the disadvantage or the risk of others. Her servants, who were all devoted to her, assured her that they feared nothing, and would, if necessary, lay down their lives to save hers; but the proprietor of the house which she occupied, on being informed of her intention, took the information in a far different spirit. He declared that the consequences of the Duchess's flight would fall upon him, and that if Madame de Doudeauville left his house he would instantly denounce her. She was obliged to relinquish her project, and to resign herself to the prolonged anguish of indefinite separation from her husband, which was all the more poignant from the awakening of an abortive hope.

A short time afterwards this brave lady, impelled by her noble generosity, exposed herself to the gravest peril.

The Abbé de Thiollaz, whom she had known at Annécy, was arrested at Bordeaux, at the height of the revolutionary period, just as he was on the point of embarking for England. The Duchesse de Doudeauville, being informed of his detention, and that it was resolved to banish him to Guiana, wrote immediately to a person of her acquaintance, to entreat that the Abbé might be set at liberty; and she also remitted three thousand francs to be handed to the Abbé from her. This letter, which was unsigned, was taken to the Hôtel de Mouchy, and discovered there in the course of a domiciliary visit, of which event Madame de Doudeauville was speedily informed. She instantly called one of her servants, and asked him if he would accompany her to the revolutionary tribunal? "Surely you would not think of going there, Madame?" remonstrated the servant, who was dreadfully frightened. He found, however, that he could not shake the resolution of the Duchess, and he made up his mind to accompany her. When she reached the dreaded spot, she left Arnold at the door, and ascended alone to the audience hall of the terrible Fouquier-Tinville. He did not take any notice of her; and she stood patiently for two hours until all the "brothers and sisters" present had retired. So soon as she found herself alone with the Public Accuser, she said to him—

"I have important business to communicate to you."

"My only business is to punish the enemies of the Republic. What have you to say? Only denunciations are received here."

"I have come about a denunciation."

"Indeed! speak then, citizeness."

"I have come to make a denunciation of an unusual kind. It is myself, and myself only, whom I denounce."

"Then you come hither to seek for death!"

"I know that, but I am fulfilling a duty."

Fouquier-Tinville looked at her with surprise, and listened to her with profound attention. She narrated her story with all its details, but without mentioning any names, and concluded by saying, "If any one is to be prosecuted, it is I!" The fierce revolutionist answered her:

"Do you know that I too have a feeling heart? Why are you interested in this priest?"

"Because he is in distress."

"Ah, yes, I understand; I can feel likewise. I have saved many people myself."

Then he reassured her, told her to make her mind easy, no harm should come to any one concerned in this matter, and, seeing that she was pale and tired, he offered his arm to lead her down the staircase. That bare arm, which seemed to her to be dyed with the blood of many innocent victims, inspired the noble lady with an almost insurmountable disgust. She could not refuse the offer, which had been kindly made, but she never recalled the few moments during which her hand had rested on the arm of Fouquier-Tinville without a shudder.

On taking leave of the Public Accuser, the Duchess gave him her name and address, so that he might know where to find her in case of need. He renewed his assurances to her that she might regard the matter as concluded. He was as good as his word. The Abbé de Thiollaz was immediately liberated; had the three thousand francs given to him, and sailed for England. This distinguished ecclesiastic retained throughout his life an ardent friendship for his benefactress. As a pledge of his gratitude he sent her a reliquary, which contained relics of St. François de Sales, and of his beloved pupil St. Jeanne Françoise de Chantal, well knowing that he could offer the Duchess nothing more precious.*

With the knowledge that there was a duty to be done or a service to be rendered, the courage of this sensitive and delicate woman rose to intrepidity; and such circumstances brought out the firmness of character which, though always united with the utmost modesty, overcame every obstacle.

Thus, when her estates were sequestrated, she demanded an investigation of her rights, and bravely defended her interests, which were those of her children and the poor. She was informed that the furniture of the Château de

* See Note B.

Montmirail was about to be sold, on the pretext that, her husband being an *emigré*, one-half of the goods which he and she owned in common should be confiscated for the benefit of the State. She immediately presented herself before the local tribunal, proved that she had been married under the *régime dotal,* or, as it would be expressed in English, that her property—of which the Château de Montmirail and its contents formed a portion— had been settled upon herself; and won her cause.

After a year's imprisonment, the Vicomtesse de la Rochefoucauld was released, and hastened to the Duchess, who received her with the utmost joy. Madame de Montesquiou, the sister of Madame de Doudeauville, had the consolation of receiving frequent visits from her, a privilege all the more dear that, not only did she during this terrible period "dwell in the midst of alarms," but she had the misfortune to lose her little daughter Rozamée. This charming child, who was so pious and charitable, that she delighted in giving away her clothes to poor children, was much attached to the Duchesse de Doudeauville. A relative said to her, one day, on leaving her, "What shall I bring you back from Paris?" and the dear child answered promptly, "Bring me back my aunt."

It pleased God to recall this little angel to Himself at the age of eight years; she knew she was going to heaven, and when she felt that death drew near, she said to her mother, "Go away now, mamma; I am going to sleep." The poor mother withdrew, and the child awoke no more. On hearing of her niece's death, Madame de Doudeauville went from Wissous to Maupertuis, in a country cart, to console her sister. While she dried the tears of Madame de Montesquiou, she little thought that in a few years she herself would have to weep for the most loving and the most beloved of daughters.

About this time the Duchess placed her son Sosthenes under the care of the Abbé Legris-Duval, a selection which proved fortunate for the boy's education. Hitherto, owing chiefly to the troublous times, he had had indifferent teachers; but his new tutor was as highly distinguished for intellectual as for moral excellence. The Abbé quickly won the heart of his young pupil, and became the beloved and devoted friend of the whole family, from whom he never afterwards separated himself, and all whose joys and sorrows he shared. "Until the hour of his death," says the Duc de Doudeauville, "he formed the delight and the edification of our home."

The zeal of the Duchess for the welfare of souls was not limited to her own family circle and household. Wherever she saw a soul in darkness, through ignorance or contact with impiety, the spectacle caused her acute pain, and she seized with avidity upon any opportunity of leading such wanderers to the knowledge and the love of truth. She was but rarely met with resistance. Her compassion was strongly aroused for Madame Helvétius, who had lost her daughter, and fallen into such a state of utter dejection that her friends despaired of inducing her to return to the routine of ordinary life; and as religion was a sealed book for her, she had nothing whereon to rest her grief-laden heart. Madame de Trans felt very deeply for the bereaved and afflicted mother; she frequently visited her, but as she herself could not venture to address Madame

Helvétius in the language of faith, she occasionally sent a nun to inquire about the state of her health, hoping that the good sister might contrive to slip in a word about God in her visits to the unfortunate woman. The device failed. Madame Helvétius would not allow the nun to gain access to her, but remained in awful solitude of soul, devoid of hope, and therefore of consolation. Madame de Trans related her vain efforts to the Duchesse de Doudeauville, and she, deeply affected by this picture of misery present and eternal, proposed to Madame de Trans that she (the Duchess) should go to Madame Helvétius, with a message from her friend, in the assumed character of a waiting-maid. A costume for the occasion was readily supplied, and Madame de Doudeauville set off on her pious errand. She rang at the door, announced that she came from Madame

de Trans, and requested permission to speak with the invalid. There was some hesitation, and at length she was about to be dismissed by the nurse in attendance on Madame Helvétius. Happily a half-open door enabled the patient to overhear the discussion, and she was struck by the soft voice, and the discreet yet earnestly anxious entreaties of her friend's messenger. She directed that the visitor should be admitted, bade her be seated, looked attentively at her, and soon satisfied herself that the person before her was no waiting-maid. The conversation went on, the Duchess with exquisite tact approached the subject of that sorrow which she would fain have alleviated. The invalid, who knew her noble visitor by reputation, quickly divined her identity, and cried out, in great agitation—
"You are the Duchesse de Doudeauville! She only could speak thus." From that

moment all strangeness ceased; the bereaved mother gave free course to her tears and to her regrets; she felt no restraint with this woman, whose heart answered to her own. The thought of God as the true and only Consoler, was not repulsed by the poor soul who had so long wandered in error and darkness, but of course it could be only vague and dim as yet. The Duchess promised to come again, she did so, and yet again. By degrees the day dawned, the light grew, and grace became more and more pressing. Madame de Doudeauville spoke of the necessity for confession, and went herself in search of a priest. Before he could fulfil his sacred office, the convert testified her confidence in her noble and saintly friend by revealing to her all the faults of her life, in anticipation of her confession to the priest. Madame Helvétius thenceforth regarded Madame de Doudeauville with undying gratitude, as the messenger of God through whom faith, peace, and hope had reached her soul.

In the meantime, the political horizon of France had cleared; in the misfortunes of the country there had come a breathing space. At the commencement of the year 1797 the armies of the Coalition ceased to be formidable. Bonaparte was restoring its former military prestige to France, and the foreign powers were already suing for peace.

The nation, which had regained its senses, was deeply desirous to efface the stain of blood with which it had been marked in the terrible year 1793; and the reawakening of France was complete when a certain deputy, on the very day of his entry among the Five Hundred, appealed for liberty for Catholic worship, and abolition of the laws which had been enacted against the clergy. The motion was heard with patience by all, and warmly applauded by many; and the Chamber voted the new decree on the 24th August 1797.

This afforded a real earnest of good things for the future. Several persons took advantage of it to cross the frontier and visit their exiled relatives and friends. The Duchesse de Doudeauville was among this number: she left Paris on the 31st August 1797, on a long journey, some particulars of which we learn from a letter of Ernestine's which has happily been preserved. The Duchess's daughter was at this time fifteen years old.

"There are circumstances in life, my dear cousin," she says, "in which one can neither speak nor write to those whom one loves; but I know from my own experience that there are none in which one does not think of them.

"If our troubles are softened by friendship, surely the joys which it shares are all the more delightful. You may easily imagine how much I miss you, how much I long to be able to open my heart to you. You knew all my regrets, why can you not witness all my happiness! How I wish I could really give you an account of all I have seen, thought, and felt.

"We left Paris, as you know, on Wednesday, the 31st August, at four in the morning. My little note will have assured you that you were not forgotten even in the hurry of our departure; although I could not describe the feelings with which I set out on a journey which was to take me to my father. I was a little child when he left us, but I had always retained the tenderest remembrance of him, and my regret for his absence had increased with my own capacity to understand and to feel.

"Our guide did not reach the first post until an hour and a half after we had arrived there. How long the time appeared to me! All sorts of fears came into my imagination; I did not understand the cause of the delay, and I was afraid the journey was to be given up after all. At length we saw the carriages in the distance, and we were soon consoled for having had to wait. While we were lamenting the delay, our people were getting a wheel repaired, which would, had its unsafe condition been unperceived, have come off after a while, and we should have been upset on the road. By nine o'clock next morning we reached Auxerre, where we were to have slept the preceding night. In order to make up for the time, which, as Sosthenes says, 'is always getting lost,' it was agreed that we should travel all the next night. We stopped, however, to sup on the way, as my mother thought that, not having dined, we ought to make at least one meal in the day. I could not tell you how many places we have passed through, but I must confess that the forests seemed very dismal to me, and my fear of them kept me broad awake. We arrived at Auxonne at nightfall, and the postmaster refused to let us have horses. There was a hot dispute about the matter, and the municipality was appealed to. The question was happily decided in our favour, and we set off, with postilions very much out of temper.

"We had hardly got clear of the town when we perceived three men following our carriage; after a while they left us, and pursued the other, which was a good distance ahead. How frightened I was! It was very dark, we were passing through a very lonely district, and, as fear magnifies everything, I kindly informed my mother that 'now we were in the middle of a wood!' There was not a vestige of such a thing! However, I was not the only one who was frightened. Only think of your cousin, who is afraid of thieves in the middle of Paris in a securely-shut house, finding herself all of a sudden in the open country, with surly postilions, and in a carriage with only women in it. Sosthenes was in the other carriage; had he been in ours, I should not have dared to be afraid. Nothing worse than fright, however, befell us.

"New difficulties awaited us at Dôle; the gates were closed, and we had to resign ourselves to passing the night in an inn outside the town. It was one o'clock when we arrived, and everybody was in bed and asleep. A sullen-looking girl opened the door to us at last, grudgingly enough, and, as all the bedrooms were occupied, she lodged us in a narrow gallery where four not particularly clean beds were ranged with their heads against the wall, like a ward in a hospital; and very thankful we were for such quarters. We had two chairs among four of us, and had to put our candle on the ground because there was no table; nevertheless we were better off than we should have been in the street.

"M. Filietaz took Sosthenes into his room, which was larger, if no cleaner than ours, but the term of probation was not very long for any of us, for at half-past three we were made to get up, in order that we might be ready to start at five. I have not yet left off grieving over those precious lost hours of sleep. We soon arrived at Poligny, the first town of the Canton of the Jura. I cannot give you an idea of the impression which Switzerland made upon me. It is a magical country of majestic mountains; on all sides were rugged rocks, deep precipices, rushing torrents, gigantic pine-trees, and then, without any apparent transition, we were in the midst of fields covered with peaceful grazing flocks, of cheerful cottages, and cultivated lands. Although Morez is not the frontier, it is the customs' station. We had to exhibit all our worldly goods, and when everything had been thoroughly examined and pulled about, leaden seals were affixed to our luggage, and by the aid of a little judicious bribery we got through and away. We had hardly passed the French boundary, when M. Filietaz stopped his carriage, got out and came to tell us, with tears in his eyes, that we were on Swiss territory. I was in the greatest delight, and I fancied that all the Swiss people looked as happy as I felt. We were approaching Nyon; at which place there was just

a chance that we might find my father.
We stopped at the inn, where Madame
Filietaz was awaiting the arrival of her
husband; but before he had spoken two
words to her, he came to tell us that the
one we hoped to see was not there. Then,
far more taken up with our concerns
than with his own, he procured horses
to take us on at once to Lausanne.
Unfortunately, a tall personage named
Prévost made his appearance, and while
he pretended to feel very much for us,
declared that we must not think of resuming our journey on that day, because we
could not possibly reach Lausanne until
midnight, and should have to arouse my
father from his sleep. My mother made
very light of that objection, but M.
Prévost proceeded to represent to her
that our nocturnal arrival would be
noised abroad in the town, and that such
notoriety might be mischievous. This

argument was decisive, and it was settled that we should not start until the next day at sunrise. I was very angry with the sympathetic M. Prévost who so pitilessly deferred our happiness. The morning dawned, however, and after a journey of a few leagues, we saw Lausanne before us. On reaching the gates we got out of the carriage, and M. Prévost led us on foot through a portion of the town, but he would not tell me whether we were 'near the place' or not. At last he took us, still keeping profound silence, up a dark staircase to a fourth story, where he knocked at a low door. Here he suddenly left us, the door was opened, and I found myself in my father's arms. Need I try to tell you what I felt? No, your own tenderness of heart will enable you to divine it, and such feelings are only weakened by an attempt to express them."

That was indeed a happy meeting to all who took part in it. M. de Doudeauville writes of it as follows :—

"The happiness which I felt on this occasion is not to be told. We had been separated for five years, and I had almost begun to despair of ever seeing my loved ones again. I passed my days in enjoying the wonderful change in my life; in listening to the stories which each and all of my dear travellers had to tell me, in learning the details of all that her courage, good sense, and tenderness had inspired the best of mothers to do for the welfare of our children. I was never tired of making them repeat everything that they had already told me, and even all that I had known before they left France, whither my thoughts constantly tended. Now I had, so to speak, no eyes, ears, or heart except to collect together, to know thoroughly, and assimilate to myself that past which I had not shared."

At the end of two months it became necessary for the husband and father once more to part with the wife and children. Madame de Doudeauville's presence was indispensable to the preservation of her large estates, and her husband could not set foot upon French soil without danger. The little party broke up, with great pain and grief, the Duke promising to remain quietly where he was until he should receive a trustworthy intimation that he might return to his own country with safety. He had not, however, the courage to abide by this resolution, but shortly afterwards, availing himself of the passport of a Swiss merchant, he succeeded in entering France. He braved many dangers, resorted to several stratagems, and ultimately arrived at Orleans, where he went to a reading-room, and read aloud, to a numerous auditory, the following sentence:—" The penalty of death is again pronounced upon all emigrants. Any such person being recognised and arrested, will be shot within the space of twenty-four hours."

The Duchess had hurried away to meet her husband, feeling much more alarm than gladness; and although the perfectly tranquil state of mind in which she found him reassured her at first, the relief lasted for only two days. On the third she was warned that the Duke had been denounced to the authorities, and she earnestly implored him to depart without a moment's delay. Her husband could not resist her terrified entreaties, and left her at once, taking with him a work of St. François de Sales, which she put into his hands at parting, to console him on his way.

The Duchess was greatly affected by

this incident, and worn out by the emotions which it caused. She therefore determined to make a retreat, to repose her mind for ten undisturbed days in the sole presence of God. In order to secure perfect quiet, she went every morning to the convent of the Filles-Dieu, near the Porte St. Dennis, and remained there until evening, when she returned to her little household. Her solitary hours reminded her of those which she had enjoyed at the memorable epoch of her first communion, with their mingling of holy wishes, sacred delights, prophetic warnings, and pious resignation. Many years had elapsed since then, and now, in the prime of her life, no longer with a vague presentiment, but with the full knowledge of the meaning and the extent of the sacrifice, this woman of noble and generous soul renewed her self-oblation, asking of God in return only that His name might be hallowed, that His kingdom might come, that His will might be done. As though to prove to her that her offering was accepted, the Holy Spirit inspired the Superior of the convent to present the Duchess, as a memento of her retreat, with a precious reliquary containing relics of the True Cross and of the Sacred Crown of Thorns.

At this time Madame de Doudeauville's mind was much engaged in the serious consideration of her daughter's future. Ernestine was now in her seventeenth year, and her mother was desirous of arranging a suitable marriage for her, impelled no doubt to this seemingly premature step by the uncertain state of affairs in France, and the prolonged absence of the head of the family. How much longer the separation of the Duke from his wife and children might last it was impossible to foresee, and the careful mother, who would never have been parted from her daughter had she consulted her own feelings only, was anxious that she should have the guidance and support of a husband, in her almost fatherless position.

Before the time came at which her daughter was to be placed in other hands, the Duchess wrote certain counsels for her use, which reveal not only the tenderness of the mother, but the ardent and enlightened faith of the strong-souled Christian. These counsels are so wise and valuable, that it has been thought well to reproduce them here, because they may serve as a model for moral and spiritual instruction; and also because they enable us, better than any description which could be given in the words of another, to understand what manner of woman she was who wrote them. She prescribes nothing that she had not practised to a far higher degree. The reflections which she suggests to her daughter formed the habitual nourishment of her own soul; the sentiments with which she strove to inspire Ernestine were those which filled her own heart, and governed all her own actions. It was thus that she loved and served God and her neighbour, but with this difference, that she gave in all its fulness that which her prudence led her to impose upon others with moderate reserve. She knew no rest, no pause in the exercise of the Christian virtues, but went valiantly on her way, growing daily in humility and charity.

The young girl to whom the following counsels are addressed was intelligent, vivacious, and of a frank, unselfish, generous nature. She was richly endowed with the qualities which bless the domestic circle, and only too rich in those which charm the world. She had been perfectly well brought up, but her accomplishments, even her fine qualities, had in them a seductive danger, as we learn from the fears which her mother expresses; so true is it that it is not sufficient that God should labour directly, and those who represent Him should labour with Him for our sanctification. That is a personal work, one which must cost us individual pains and toil—" And of him to whom much has been given, the Master will require much."

CHAPTER V.

COUNSELS TO A DAUGHTER.

"You will think it strange, my dear Ernestine, that having you always before my eyes, I should yet feel it necessary to write to you. But I know that your pleasure will be as great in receiving such a proof of my solicitude as that solicitude is pressing and constant. Your heart is always open to my counsels, and I do not doubt that they will affect you more strongly when you have them in my own handwriting, even though they should be opposed to your tastes and inclinations. There are certain points on which I had intended to reserve my advice until you should have been a little older, but the new state of life on which you are soon to enter demands that I should speak without reserve or delay.

"I am therefore about to open my mind freely to you, to let you read in my soul all the hopes which I found on the work which the grace of God has done in yours, the virtues whose full bloom I have a right to expect from the germs that rejoiced my heart in your childhood, and also the qualities which your happily gifted intelligence, and lofty tenderness of nature, ought to develop in you to a very high degree. I will not disguise any of my apprehensions from you, although I do not intend to allow you to see their full extent; because as you are not yet a mother you could not comprehend all that motherhood implies, its happiness, its griefs, its joys, and its fears.

"I will also make my confession to you; it is needful for my own peace of mind. I am far from attributing the defects which I discern in you to yourself. No, my dear child, it was my inexperience when I had to commence your education, that is to blame for the errors in your training; I accuse my own defects, my own want of strength and firmness; they prevented the full outpouring of the Divine blessing upon you. Take this conviction of mine into your mind, and you will be able to judge of the importance which I attach to this attempt at fortifying you in advance against certain dangers which alarm me, perhaps too easily; and you will also pardon me if I exaggerate a little. You must see in all that I am about to say to you only the tenderness of a Christian mother who trembles at the approach of a parting with her beloved daughter.

Picture to yourself a merchant who is entrusting his treasure to the sea, the fruit of his labours and his watchings, his only hope; he sees at once in his mind's eye the port at which he longs that his precious freight should have arrived, and also the many dangers of the voyage. The rushing of the waves which may swallow up his treasure is in his ears; think of his suspense, and you may form an imperfect idea of the anguish and the perplexity of your mother's heart. One sole thought has the power to ease that heart; it is, that I have always known you to be truly religious, full of firm and living faith. I will not say of piety, because your present mode of life does not actually deserve to be called pious; but, if you persevere, this precious gift will be given to you as a reward, and will clear the path in which your feet are already set.

"My only desire is, that you should adhere to those solid and practical religious exercises, without which your faith would soon become enfeebled. Should that occur, the world, and those who are on the side of the world in the great conflict, would speedily acquire influence over you; their maxims would no longer seem strange to you; by degrees they would become pleasing, and they would end by leading you astray. Then, human respect, which has already had some victories over you, would precipitate your defeat. I pause here, my beloved child; I could not contemplate the terrible prospect of such a misfortune; you can avoid it by reviving and strengthening your faith by the practice of our holy religion. Apply yourself to the comprehension of all that it requires of you, and of all that it promises you. I am the more ardently desirous to encourage you in this study, that it will afford you the only means of finding lasting happiness for yourself, and of procuring that happiness for all who may depend upon you. You might, indeed, without the celestial aid of religion, secure some passing enjoyments and pleasures, and even confer the same on others; but with what a difference! How dearly you would purchase those fleeting hours! Your enjoyment would never be free from disquiet, your pleasure would never be unaccompanied by remorse. The happiness which I desire for you, and which religion affords, having its source in purity of heart, and in the peace of the soul which comes from that purity, can never be troubled by external events, or determined by worldly circumstances. It will shed its charm over your whole life. The world may be overturned, empires may be destroyed, nations may rend each other, but no human power can ever rob us of that priceless possession, and with it all evils are endurable. It is not a mere sentimental impression which makes me speak thus to you; this is the fruit of my lifelong experience. Oh that I could communicate to your mind the conviction which has been impressed upon mine! Those who have gone through the French Revolution and survived it, cannot entertain any doubt of the nothingness of the things of this world. I have seen honours and dignities vanish away, and with them those who enjoyed them; I have seen the greatest, the safest fortunes annihilated; great names dragged in the mire; brilliant reputations branded with shame; the most beneficent institutions abolished; finally, the throne and the altar overthrown. I have seen men intoxicated with the splendour of a glittering dream, sacrificing their health, their peace, and their conscience to it, and in eight years not a trace of it existed any more. Amid this total overthrow, how often has my soul been forced to acknowledge, 'Thou only art great, O my God, Thou only art sure and stable, Thou only canst promise and confer a lasting happiness. Every human stay to which I clung has crumbled under my touch. Thou alone remainest, but with Thine aid I can endure all.'

"Do you, then, my dear child, give the first years which are yours to dispose of, to God, unshared, and without a rival. Your childhood was consecrated to Him, do you, in the exercise of your free will, consecrate your youth to Him, and do not doubt the liberality with which the God of all Goodness will reward your sacrifices and sustain your faltering steps.

When once you have set out upon the way in which He would have you walk, He will be careful to smooth all its difficulties, and He will make the second portion of His precept—the love of our neighbour—easy for you to fulfil. You will find His work everywhere, and in all persons, and you will respect it, above all in the unhappy, in the indigent, in those who are destitute of the temporal advantages under which life presents itself to you, those for whom the Eternal Father reserves consolation in the life to come, which shall recompense them for the neglect and abandonment they have endured in this world. What ought you not to render to the Lord for that He has placed in your hands so simple a means of expiating those faults which are inseparable from the enjoyment of wealth, and of indulging the suggestions of your own kind heart at the same time. You will recognise the authority of God in that of your superiors, and you will find it easy to render them the submission and consideration which are their due.

"Your rule over your inferiors should have no harshness in it; your empire should be that of kindness. Exact impartiality being your law, no prejudice should ever influence your actions, or favour have any access to you. You should rather seek out those who keep themselves in the background. Thus will all feel your wisdom and indulgence, and render thanks to God, whose servant you are.

"In all human beings you will behold His image; and they will find you ever ready to assist them. You will set up no rivalry with your equals; you will rejoice in their welfare, and their successes will become yours. Looking upon yourself as a member of one great family, all of whom are destined to a similar career and aspire to the same end; the glory of its Head and the happiness of all will be the animating motives of your life.

"How, then, should you not spread the fame and kindle the love of this holy religion? Who knows whether God, in order to encourage your feeble efforts and to reward your sacrifices, may not make use of you to rescue souls who are on the point of forsaking Him, or to raise up some who have already fallen. Ah, my dear child, if He should grant you this grace, all your life would not suffice for the thanksgiving you will owe to Him. How admirable are His ways when He uses such weak instruments to work His miracles of mercy, and how happy are they whom He thus deigns to employ! Hold your heart, then, always in readiness to accept of every demand which He may make upon you. And now let us examine the general and special obstacles which you will have to encounter.

"I do not disguise or deny that religion exacts many sacrifices; I know, and I have only too thoroughly experienced, that we are born with an inclination towards evil very difficult to be surmounted, and that before we reach the state of peace and calm of which I have already spoken, we have many battles to fight, many victories over ourselves to gain; but, I would ask you, whether, even apart from religion, you do not feel it both desirable and necessary to conquer the passions which otherwise might master you?

You are in the habit of praising that merely human courage which frequently leads to fatal results; do you not think there is greatness of mind, true elevation of character, in acquiring a clear insight into one's own motives and a complete mastery over one's own actions. It seems to me that the greatest conqueror is nothing beside the simple and honest man who has made himself his constant study, and self-conquest his greatest glory, who, having acquired the habit of self-repression, suffers little from the ill-regulated impulses of his nature, and can at any moment decide upon a line of action without being blinded by the impetuosity of his passions.

"The philosophers endeavoured to make us believe that they had attained to this desirable condition. Religion not only gives me the means of attaining to the same condition, while it shows me my need of it; but it also makes me love self-sacrifice, because in self-sacrifice it indicates that the way to heaven lies.

Ah, how much more we may learn from a short meditation on the Life and Passion of our Divine Lord, than from all the arguments of cold and formal reasoning, which, indeed, tell us what we ought to do, but give us no strength for the doing of it. It is from your crucifix, my child, that you will learn in what solid good really consists; then you will better appreciate that which the world has to offer you, and you will have no trouble or pain in detaching yourself from it. In contemplating the cross every illusion vanishes; and when the heart has once taken in its truth, nothing else has any attraction for it. At the foot of the cross you will learn how heavy is the chain with which the world binds us, and how light and easy is the yoke of the Gospel. May our Divine Lord give you grace to carry it always, and spare you the agony of regret that you had ever hesitated between the world and Him. I could not endure the idea that you could ever reject Him, and thus force me to lament that I had given you birth. Love your Divine Master thoroughly, and you will have only one cause of disquiet —that you cannot do enough for Him. When you were a child you used to come to me and confess the little faults of which I knew nothing, with perfect confidence, and, in the ingenuousness of your heart you found consolation, and in my tenderness the peace which you had lost. Go to our Divine Lord in your womanhood as you came to me in your childhood. With what joy did I press you to my heart, how often your tears caused mine to flow, while I thought only of drying those in your dear eyes! Oh, my beloved child, let my love, my indulgence, give you a feeble notion of the love, the mercy, the tender-heartedness of your God! If you have found those things in his weak, imperfect, frail creature, what may you not expect of Him from whom they all came, who was the source of them, and who sets no bounds to His love for you, save those of His own immensity! Remember that my love, my care for you, did but increase in proportion to your weakness and your needs; and believe that the loving-kindness of your Heavenly Father is subject to the same law, exercised with the infinity of God. He is a good physician who knows all your wounds, probes their depth, measures their extent, foresees their danger, holds in His hands the remedies which will bring you relief, and is ever burning with the desire to apply them. One aspiration towards Him is sufficient to enable His justice to give free course to His mercy, and then He will pour into your soul that salutary balm which takes the smart out of every remedy, and hastens its action.

"I acknowledge to you, my beloved child, that of all the feelings which I have experienced, that of maternity, which does not detract from any other, but which surpasses them all, seems to me most fitly to represent the love of God for His creatures. I sometimes force myself to consider Him as my judge, but my thoughts always recur to Him as my Father; and however faithless I have been, however unworthy I may be to be reckoned among the number of His children, I abandon myself entirely to His love, and say to Him repeatedly, 'In Thee, O Lord, have I put my trust; I cannot be confounded; Thy word is the pledge of that.'

"May the heart of my dear child,

filled with steady and worthy hopes, be rivetted to Him who alone can fulfil them. This is a happiness of which I am too weak and too ignorant to speak, but it seems to me that a soul which has attained to detachment from the things of this world may form some slight idea of it. To love immeasurably and throughout eternity the object which is most lovable, the source of all that is good; never to have to dread the possibility of offending that object; to see with God, to feel with Him, to receive His Divine communications—what happiness!

"If, my beloved child, by my example, through my defects, perhaps through too indulgent an affection for you, I have ever given you any other impression of religion than the true one, I ask your pardon at the feet of our Lord Jesus

Christ; and there I implore of Him that the chastisement which my faults merit may not fall on you. At His feet also I solemnly protest to you that I have never formed any other wishes for you than those which tended to your growth in grace, and your secure possession of this true and only happiness.

"I remember that an instant after you were born, I offered you to God. Yes, at that moment when I was experiencing the first transport of a mother's joy, when all my sufferings seemed nothing in comparison with their reward in you, when I would have thought it only just that I should have paid with my life for the happiness of having given you yours,—even at that moment I begged of God that He would spare you to me only if you were to love Him to all eternity. He has accepted my sacrifice, and has preserved your life.

May I not hope that my heart's desire for you will be fulfilled to its utmost extent?

"I beseech Thee, O God of mercy and goodness, not to look upon the weakness of her who offers this petition to Thy Divine Majesty, but to remember only that she is interceding for a child whom Thou hast given her, and that her child is Thine also. I have never forgotten Thy rights; I have, indeed, been afraid to count her too much my own. Thou knowest that I have never asked for her the treasures of this world, nor any temporal things, but only that celestial dew of blessing whose value I know. Shed this dew in abundance upon her, O my God, Thou who alone knowest how dear she is to me. I accept all to which Thy holy will may destine her, provided only that she may remain ever faithful to Thee; and that, after having transmitted to her children the priceless heirloom of the Faith, in all its integrity, she may love and bless Thee to all eternity."

These pages were written some months before Ernestine's marriage. When the decisive hour was drawing near, the wise and tender mother gave a more precise form to her far-sighted counsels.

"Paris, 15*th May* 1798.

"You ask me, my dear Ernestine, to construct a rule of life for you, to draw up a plan for the distribution and employment of your time. When you first made this request of me, I refused compliance with it, because I was deeply conscious of my own insufficiency for the task, and also because I thought it would be more advantageous that you should lay down a rule for yourself. On second thoughts, however, I am so deeply touched by your confidence in me that

I am about to fulfil your wish, after having humbly besought the aid of the Holy Spirit.

"The regulation of one's time by a formal rule has been enjoined by the masters of the spiritual life, by Fénélon, Saint François de Sales, and many others, and consecrated by their own practice. They have always prescribed it to those who desire to lead a Christian life, to avoid offending God, and to make progress in virtue. I am quite convinced that many and great graces are attached to this observance. At the time of my marriage, although I was very young, I felt the necessity for a rule of life, and I derived great benefit from that which I concocted in my own head (aged fourteen!), and which was afterwards modified by a wise director. My knowledge of your character, my dear child, leads me to believe this special practice indispensable to your safety and happiness.

"Pious practices have but little charm for you; you dread those in which there is restraint and subjection; you have adopted, without exactly knowing why, a prejudice against what you call petty observances; and these are just the reasons which render it necessary that you should prescribe certain practices to yourself, with a firm resolution to adhere to them. It is precisely because you dislike 'small' things that you must imbue your motives with the supernatural, and regard it as utterly beneath you to be led by your own humours or caprice.

"When you shall have adopted a rule of life, it will fulfil this object, and procure the advantages to which I allude. Each action will then bear the stamp of obedience, and that is the surest way to attain, even without knowing it yourself, to the highest perfection. But I must not longer defer the detail of the obligations which will be imposed upon you, because I can perceive that your youthful courage is daunted by my exordium, and although your reason asks for this rule, you dread it; you think it can only be practicable in the religious life, and you shrink from its supposed severity. It is, therefore, deeply important that you should have it proved to you that religion adapts itself to the weakness of our age, our health, and even of our character; that it asks nothing of us that is not reasonable, and does but consecrate our ordinary duties.

THE EMPLOYMENT OF THE DAY.

" 1. Remain eight hours in your bed. At your age that is the proportion of rest which is necessary for you. Your hour for retiring must, therefore, be regulated by your hour for rising; but except in the case of indisposition, or of some unusual fatigue, be careful not to exceed the eight hours.

" 2. Let your first thought on awaking be for God. Offer all your actions during the day to Him, and invoke your guardian angel.

" 3. Immediately after you are dressed say your morning prayers. Select them from the *Journée Chrétienne*, or adopt a shorter form if you like; but when you have made your selection, adhere to it.

" 4. Read a chapter of 'The Imitation of Christ,' and pass a quarter of an hour in meditation upon it. At present you will find the first and second books most beneficial to you.

" 5. Hear Mass every day.

" 6. Devote an hour or an hour and a

half to breakfast, and the attentions which it will be your duty to render to your husband's family.

"7. Devote two hours during the morning to reading history or travels, or to taking lessons from your various masters. If you would render your reading really profitable, make extracts.

" 8. Reserve one half hour for the reading of a religious book, and before you begin, lift up your heart to God in prayer, that He may give you grace to profit by it.

"9. When you dress for dinner, endeavour to pass as little time at your toilet as possible. Take advantage of this necessary occupation to commit to memory some well selected pieces of poetry; thus you will cultivate your memory and adorn your mind. Such a habit will also prevent your being too much absorbed in that dangerous occupation for young persons, the study of the fashions.

"10. I should like you to make it your custom to reflect, for five minutes before dinner, on the manner in which you have employed your morning, and carried out your rule.

"11. During dinner, while you make yourself as agreeable as possible to your relatives, try to lift up your heart to God from time to time. It would be well that you should not allow any meal to pass without some little act of mortification. At present, limit yourself to repressing your too numerous fancies; and do not at any time overstrain this precept, although you will derive great advantage to your health from obedience to it.

"12. After dinner, remain with your relatives for two hours; employ this time in needlework, and endeavour to make it pass agreeably to others by pleasant conversation.

"13. Retire to your own apartments for two hours, or two hours and a half, during which recite two decades of the rosary, and one of the penitential psalms, so that in the course of a week you shall have said the entire rosary and the seven psalms. Employ the remainder of that interval in reading, writing, and the study of music and drawing.

"13. The evening may be devoted to your friends, and to society, according to the tastes and wishes of your husband.

"14. Observe at supper similar rules to those which have been laid down for you during dinner.

"15. Say your night prayers, make your examination of conscience, and after having asked God to pardon the faults of the day, and thanked Him for its graces, try to fall asleep, thinking good thoughts.

"16. Your confessor only can regulate the number of your communions; nevertheless I should wish you to form a resolution that you will never allow more than a month to elapse without approaching the Holy Sacrament, and if you make it a regular practice to go to confession every fortnight, that solemn duty will become easy to you.

"Three days before you receive Holy Communion, read a chapter of 'The Imitation,' one of those in the fourth book; watch over yourself with redoubled vigilance; fulfil your duties with greater exactitude, and always bear in mind that God requires from us the free service of the heart.

"Keep away from any amusement that could distract your thoughts, unless there should be some legitimate reason for your joining in it; your husband's wishing you to do so would be such a reason.

"Continue the reading of the fourth book of 'The Imitation,' for three days after your communion, and watch carefully over yourself, as a thanksgiving.

"It would be well that you should do some acts of charity, in addition to your habitual almsgiving, before you approach the sacraments.

"This rule, which is a good one for the present, because it is compatible with all your duties, may at a later period cease to be suitable for you; in that case it might be modified. It will be sufficient, that you promise to change nothing in it without advice, but you will do well to submit for consideration, and even to propose, such alterations as, in the course of circumstances, may seem to you to be right and reasonable. I am now about to set down for you a few general rules, which, by placing several points clearly before your mind, may enable you to avoid disquietude.

FIRST GENERAL RULE.

"As the first of all rules, that indeed upon which the salvation of our souls depends, is the fulfilment of our duty, it is of course understood that the distribution of your time is always to be subject to the will and pleasure of your husband. Whenever his presence interrupts one of your religious exercises, you must never appear annoyed, but promptly discontinue even a prayer in which you might be finding the utmost consolation. You should be always animated by a desire to render goodness and piety attractive in his eyes, and in order that they may be so, you must endeavour to correct those small faults in your disposition which would interfere with this object. When your religious exercises are interrupted, either by your husband or for any other reason independent of your own will, you must not be uneasy, and in order to avoid confusion, you will do well to resume the employment of your time on the moment. Be careful, however, to allot the few prayers and the short reading which I have prescribed, to those hours during which you may reckon most securely upon being uninterrupted.

SECOND GENERAL RULE.

" When you want to decide upon what you ought to do in matters that cannot be included in this rule of life, ask yourself whether the action or the thing you are about to undertake, is one you can offer up to Almighty God.

RULES FOR ALMSGIVING.

"On each occasion of your receiving your allowance, set apart the portion of the poor in the first place. Fix that portion at one-tenth of the sum at your disposal. I take it for granted that you will never contract any debts, otherwise you could not give away money, for it would not be honest to do so.

"Endeavour to distribute your alms with discernment, giving preference to old people, to the infirm, and to those who are more especially consecrated to God.

"If, without omitting any duty, or committing any imprudence, you can visit the sufferers whom you aid, in person, to console them by evincing interest in them, and lead them to venerate religion and the God of charity, whose instrument for their service you are, you will derive great satisfaction from doing so, and you will only have to place a restraint upon a too merely human impulse of generosity. I have no doubt that in such a case you would add a little to the sum I have already named as the fixed portion of the poor, something that you had intended to expend upon a new fashion, or a superfluous ornament, and a sacrifice of this kind will not be wanting in importance.

RULES FOR YOUR CHOICE OF BOOKS.

"A rule for one's reading is of great moment at every age, but of especial importance in youth, when, as all one's impressions are more keen and vivid, an ill-judged selection may have disastrous results. I do not, however, intend to make any reference to such books as are contrary to religion or morality, nor even to romances. Every Christian has renounced reading of this kind in his baptism, and the principles by which I know you to be animated would, at any rate, fill you with horror of it; but more than this is needful for you. Propose to yourself as an invariable rule to take advice before reading any religious book. A certain work may be positively good, and useful at one particular time, but dangerous at another. The director to whom God has entrusted the care of your soul will be given grace to decide for you in these matters.

"As for books of instruction and amusement, it will be well that you should not trust your own judgment in the choice of them either; but have recourse to the advice of pious and enlightened persons."

Ernestine de la Rochefoucauld became the wife of the Marquis de Rastignac. The prudent mother would not commit her child's future to the hands of one of the brilliant, unprincipled, frivolous men who abounded in French society at that epoch : she selected a man of upright mind and serious tastes, with a strict sense of duty, and whose practical piety was a guarantee for the peace and happiness of his home.

Notwithstanding the fearful calamities through which the French nation had recently passed, in spite of the horrors which Paris had lately witnessed, the frivolous city was again rushing into every sort of amusement and dissipation. To a looker-on it must have seemed as though the world of wealth, fashion, and vanity were intoxicating themselves with pleasure, in order to get rid of the recollection of the blood of the Martyrs, which was hardly yet dry. The Marquise de Rastignac (aged seventeen) was one of the most popular and eagerly-sought of the brilliant throng; her personal attractions, her vivacity, her wit, and her high spirits rendered her an idol of society, and in this there lurked a great danger. At Ernestine's age a woman's head is easily turned, and it is always delightful to be loved, and made much of. Her disposition was peculiarly amiable and confiding, and she was incapable of suspecting the malignity of the world which is as envious as it is flattering. Conscience, however, rebuked her; she heard the inward whisper, "God is not satisfied, He asks other things than these." She carried her burthen to her mother; with loving filial confidence she confided to that tried and faithful friend troubles many a young woman similarly placed would not have acknowledged even to herself. Sure of finding in her the double aid of strength and tenderness, she joyfully sought the sure refuge of sanctity and love.

The Duchess writes to her daughter, under the double impression of alarm and thankfulness, in the following terms, which convey fresh counsels combined with earnest entreaties:—

"MONTMIRAIL, 28*th December* 1799.

"Our recent conversations, my dear Ernestine, were full of consolation for me; and yet the satisfaction I derived from them has made your departure all the more painful to me. Nevertheless, I like to tell you how sweet and welcome are the impressions which they have left behind, and what rest of heart and mind I derive from them. The insight into yourself, which God, in His great mercy, has granted you—an inestimable grace —frequently withheld from persons much older than you are—the fulness of your confidence in me, and, even more than these, the teachableness of your spirit, fill me with hope. Yes, my beloved child, I am happy about you, but a mother's heart veers rapidly from hope to fear, and I feel it necessary to explain to you the reasons that cause these alternations in mine. May God grant that my advice may be profitable to you. The apprehensions I feel, and which I believe to be well founded, may seem to you premature; if so, let them be justified in your eyes by your mother's love.

"You complain of the weakness in your character that makes you appear to agree with the opinions of whomsoever is speaking to you, and hinders you from protesting, except in the case of downright unmistakeable evil or wrong; you are conscious of a desire to please, of a certain coquetry of the intelligence that leads you to seek the society and the admiration of persons who are superior in talent to others, because that superiority of theirs is flattering to yourself. You are inclined to general good nature; to kindness which might, indeed, be a virtue, and undoubtedly arises from the goodness of your heart; but you are conscious of a mixed motive in it, the hurtful one being your immoderate desire of the esteem and approbation of your fellows. The result is, that day by day human respect gains a greater sway over you, and the weakness to which you yield prevents you from throwing it off. The tenderness of your conscience keeps you alive to the smallest faults, but the dread of being censured, of passing for a person of narrow mind, renders you deaf to the warning voice. You suffer from this interior conflict, and then you try to believe that you are worrying yourself about things that are not really essential; that in religious matters all that is merely of counsel may be set aside, provided that all that is of precept be strictly observed; and that it is not expedient to adopt a line while one is young, to which one cannot be sure of being always able to adhere.

"You assign a certain portion to Almighty God; and then you curtail it; whereas the portion assigned to the world increases as the other diminishes, and in proportion. Nevertheless, this division does not procure you the tranquillity which you long for, for you are pursued and hemmed in by the mercy of God; you cannot look within, upon your own heart, without blushing at your weakness, without being humiliated, as you have confessed to me, by the hold it has gained upon you, and frightened at the abyss into which it may precipitate you. But, you tell me, I do no evil! Is it no evil to refuse God Almighty that which He asks; to deprive yourself of graces that are the reward of fidelity; to expose yourself, by resistance, to the loss of those graces that have already been vouchsafed to you? And, even supposing this were, indeed, doing no evil, it is at least leaving undone the good you ought, and are destined to do. The more largely God has gifted you with the love of virtue and the horror of vice, the more urgently He demands that you shall practise them both with all your heart and soul; the more serious your responsibilities are towards Him, the more culpable you become if you fail to fulfil them. Do you think, my dear Ernestine, that the loftiness of mind, the courage, the strength, even in the midst of weakness, which would render you capable of the greatest sacrifices, the gentleness and gratitude you express so sweetly ought to be restricted to the sphere of purely moral qualities, and that He who has implanted in your soul the precious germ of so many virtues has not the right to exact that they shall be exercised for Himself? Do you think that you can ever enjoy true peace while you turn those virtues aside from their right use, and hinder them from rising to the source whence they came? But you must not be hurt or alarmed because I say this to you; let those qualities be directed aright, and they will become more amiable, more attractive than ever.

"I think, my dear child, you cannot fail to recognise yourself in the picture I have just set before you, because it is an accurate reproduction of all that your ingenuous confidence has revealed to me. Upon that avowal I have founded my hopes; an evil recognised is already half cured; you will need nothing more than a firm and constant will to remedy it completely, and that you may gain by asking for it from Him whom you have so earnestly besought to abide with you.

"While I am writing to you, all my fears vanish away, my mission becomes altogether one of consolation. If I had to open your eyes to your own faults, to combat any illusions of yours, I should not be without deep distrust and dread of my inadequate powers; but, in this instance, the mercy of God has done everything beforehand. I am speaking to a soul conscious of its wretchedness — a soul shrinking with dread from the gulf of ruin towards which it is dragged—a soul, feeling itself held back by an all-powerful hand, to which it will, no doubt, surrender itself entirely and without delay. If, indeed, it were a question of disabusing your mind of the delusive charm of all the things of this world, I might be alarmed, considering your youth, and the many dangers and snares which encompass you; but, happy mother that I am, no such task is mine. You had hardly tasted of the pleasures of this world, when you learned their emptiness, their insufficiency, their nothingness. In them your heart has found nothing to satisfy itself withal. You have seen many men, and judged them; you say that *they are almost all fools*, and that the number of the wise is very small; I have, therefore, no fear lest you should sacrifice your conscience, your peace, your eternal happiness, to acquire the esteem of persons whom you despise, and of a world whose corruption fills you with horror. Laying aside for a moment the powerful motives which no doubt will determine your future course, how could I suppose that you would not prefer the approbation of that small number on whom you have conferred the appellation of 'wise,' and of whom, therefore, you must believe that they have chosen the better part? In addition to this, how easy it would be to show you that they who have done the most to deserve the vain applause of the world, are those who have most rarely obtained it!

"The world, however inconsistent it may be in its conduct, is not always so in its judgments, and its cruellest jests and raillery are directed against persons of weak character and narrow mind, who, belonging heartily neither to God nor to the world, wander about in a state of uncertainty, neither doing the good that they love, nor avoiding the evil that they fear, giving endless advantage to their spiritual enemies by their inconsistency, and reaping, as the fruit of all their pains, that general contempt which attends weakness and cowardice.

"What, then, humanly speaking, is necessary to the attainment of the esteem of men? To be consistent, to know one's own mind, and to carry out one's own purpose, to practise the virtues; for you may rest assured that the merest worldling who attacks you with his malicious jests, when he finds you are impervious, does homage in the depths of his heart to those principles against which he declaims, because they furnish his own condemnation. Your personal interest is at one with your religion, it counsels you to despise the judgments of men, while it shows you that your contempt is the surest means of obtaining their esteem. Religion asks no more than this of you, but offers in return no such barren reward. What encouragements, what hopes, what means of grace does not religion hold out to you! Ah, my child, lift up your thoughts for a moment above all created things, contemplate the blessedness of heaven, and then covet, if you can, the good things of this world! Look at the crown reserved for you, the crown promised to your courage and perseverance, and still regard with pleasure, if you can, the frivolous toys with which human beings amuse themselves here below. Let your heart be penetrated by the love of your God, and you will soon estimate the friendship and the approval of man at their proper value.

"Descend into your own heart, and you will find Him there; He calls you, He entreats you, He waits for you, and each time that you have recourse to Him, and submit yourself entirely to His Divine Will, He will send you His ineffable peace. Elsewhere, and in anything else, you will seek for tranquillity in vain.

"What is it that holds you back, my dear Ernestine? Your intelligence is perfectly convinced—nay, more, it is enlightened; your heart is touched, you are ashamed of your weakness. Are you going to yield to it anew? What have you to weigh in the balance? The jests of those who have not sufficient strength to imitate you, the sarcasms of a few unbelievers! No, my beloved child, such puerile considerations will not tempt you to hesitate; you will not indeed set yourself up as a preacher, no such office devolves upon you, and you have not acquired the right to offer instruction to others; let a consistent life, conduct strictly in accord with your principles, be your apostolate. Yes, let this be so, and be careful to add to it all that gaiety, amiability, and simplicity can do to render it more attractive, and therefore more efficacious. People who mock you will soon leave off when they find that their jests are invariably received with gentle, quiet reserve; and if you regulate your life by a steady and consistent rule, there will be nothing in it, or about you, for scoffers to take hold of. Pursue this line of conduct for two or three years, and at the end of them you will find yourself perfectly free; society, convinced that there is nothing to be gained by persecuting you, will abandon the unprofitable pastime, and will turn its malignant attention to others, who may in their turn be encouraged and sustained by your example. After a few years of oblivion you will be surprised to find those persons who affected to regard you as silly and narrow-minded, coming to consult you in difficult circumstances, sheltering themselves under the reputation which you will have acquired, and holding the interest which you evince in them and their affairs a high honour.

"Why should I, however, return even for a moment to those human motives which are not for a soul like yours to entertain, though they may, and I hope they will, afford you a momentary encouragement? If I were to plead with you upon any basis of this kind, should I not urge your demeanour to myself, your confidence, those feelings which you have so freely imparted to me; and should I need any stronger plea than my own happiness, my own satisfaction, to induce you to adopt an instant resolution? Far be it from me, however, to bid you pause there; no, my child, both you and I must be actuated by higher and purer motives, and the mother of Ernestine must render herself worthy of her daughter's confidence, by leading her to seek the only real good, the one Being to whom we ought to sacrifice all beside. Pursue, my dear child, the career which lies before you, but never lose sight of eternity, in which it must terminate; let all your actions, tending towards that end, be animated and sanctified by the blessed hope it inspires. In that eternity is the happiness my heart yearns for on your behalf; to secure it for you I would give up my peace, my life here below; there it is that I desire to possess you, to be with you, never to be parted from you again."

Notwithstanding the difference in their respective characters, Madame de Rastignac was worthy of her mother, and she well understood the language in which she addressed her. The two were alike in elevation and generosity of feeling, and

Almighty God had given them to one another, that the daughter might draw out the treasures of grace and wisdom hidden in the mother's heart, and that the mother might be a safeguard for her child against all the seductions of the heart and the fancy.

Before long a new happiness and new duties were added to the lot of the young Marquise, whose life was already so full of blessings. She hailed the birth of her little daughter Zénaïde with transports of joy, and resolved that the child should be brought up as carefully as she herself had been by the tenderest and most vigilant of mothers. Her joy on this auspicious occasion was complete when she was told that her father was about to return to France. The Duc de Doudeauville, who ardently longed to rejoin his family, had, in fact, started off on his journey homewards immediately upon receiving the news of the fall of the Directory (18 *Brumaire* 1799), without waiting for the decree of amnesty which the *émigrés* expected from the First Consul ; but on this occasion the difficulties he had to encounter beset him in foreign countries, which having been defeated by Buonaparte, were suspicious of all Frenchmen. By the help of his title of Grandee of Spain, under the name of Ambrosio, born in the vicinity of Madrid (the château de Madrid in the Bois de Boulogne being within half a league of Paris), the Duc de Doudeauville travelled as a Spaniard through Italy and Austria. He had arrived in safety at Lyons, and intended to start for Paris the next day, when he was prevented from doing so by a letter from his wife. The Duchess implored him not to incur any useless risk, but to wait until he should have received his papers before resuming his journey.

He submitted to her better judgment, not without pain, for now that the long-desired goal was so near, every minute's delay seemed an hour to him. After eight days of impatient suspense, during which no communication reached him, he could not bear it any longer, and he set off on the way to Paris. Hardly had he quitted Lyons than the Duchess arrived there, having travelled day and night from the moment she had secured the Duke's papers. She alighted at the hotel and eagerly asked for "Monsieur Ambrosio."

"Madame will require breakfast?"

"No, no, I only want Monsieur Ambrosio."

Then seeing the hostess's look of irrepressible surprise, the Duchess added, "Monsieur Ambrosio is my husband."

The hostess, taking compassion on her impatience, turned over the leaves of the register of the hotel, and showed the poor lady that after a sojourn of ten days at Lyons, M. Ambrosio had just left that city. Excessively disappointed, and unable to understand his conduct, which was entirely due, as it ultimately appeared, to a lost letter, the Duchess exclaimed, "How very strange! And what could he have been doing here?" The hostess, still mistaking the cause of her agitation, said, soothingly, "Make your mind easy, Madame, he led a very quiet life. It is true that he walked about a good deal, but only with his poodle." Notwithstanding her vexation, Madame de Doudeauville could not help laughing at this, and she assured the good woman that she had no uneasiness respecting the conduct of "Monsieur Ambrosio." She then ordered post-horses, and set off as soon as possible on her return journey.

The husband and wife met at Macon; and, notwithstanding her fatigue, and the delicate health which she was in at the time, the Duchess would not hear of any delay in their return to Paris. She could not bear to defer the happiness of her children for an hour; and as speedily as possible the whole family were reunited after their long separation.

The Holy Scriptures speak thus of the "valiant woman:" "The heart of her husband trusteth in her, and he shall have no need of spoils. She hath considered a field and bought it. Her children rose up and called her blessed, her husband, and he praised her." These words may truly be applied in the case of Madame de Doudeauville; not only had she, by her truthful courage, saved all her estates in the perilous times, "but," says the Duke, "she had beautified them by her care, and increased their value by her wise administration."

"The first time," he continues, "that

she took me to see one of our domains, she presented it to me as a conquest, with a sweet and modest pride which became her well. I, who had so long despaired of ever seeing those well-remembered scenes again—I, whose ambition during my days of exile had not soared beyond the possible retention of my gardener's house, felt as if I must be dreaming when I was reinstated as the master of all these lands.

"The beneficent fairy to whom I owed the preservation of my beloved home had had the forethought and kindness to place my former valet, whom I had sent back to France eight years before, as steward on the estate. This good man, who had known me from my childhood, embraced me with tears of joy, that made me weep likewise. This, however, was only a prelude to the happiness awaiting me at Paris, where I found my mother, my children, some other relatives, and several devoted friends. What delight, what joy, what bewildering happiness it was!"

Alas! a few pages later, we find these words: "The happiness which I enjoyed among my own belongings was not destined to a long continuance."

CHAPTER VI.

THE DEATH OF MADAME DE RASTIGNAC.

FROM the beautiful and holy life we have followed thus far, suffering has never been absent. As a charming child, a sweet and lovely girl, a brilliant court lady;—in whatever stage of life, under whatever circumstances we contemplate the Duchesse de Doudeauville, we find the shadow that worldly minds in their ignorance would fain put away, but without which we should have set before us only a commonplace picture of mere passing prosperity.

The trials of her life bring out the character of Madame de Doudeauville in additional grandeur. During the Revolutionary tempest she had to tremble for all those who were dearest to her, she experienced every kind and degree of apprehension, but it seemed as if Almighty God had been satisfied with making her contemplate and accept the worst that could befall. She was the visible angel of her family, and in her turn she was defended by a celestial protector. But at length the sword was to pierce her soul also, and she, like the Virgin Mother, for whom she had such deep veneration, had her place assigned to her at the foot of the Cross. We shall find her there, still brave and generous, her head and heart bowed down in submission to the will of God. She has braved the scaffold, but her martyrdom, that which all mothers will appreciate, still awaits her.

In the midst of her joyous life, and at the height of her domestic happiness,

Madame de Rastignac was taken suddenly ill. A troublesome and constant cough, attended by fever and general weakness, were the first symptoms of her illness, and they spread consternation among her relatives by whom Ernestine was as much beloved as she was admired and courted by society in general. Her mother, who relied on the fine air of Montmirail as the best remedy, brought her there in July 1802; but the disease, so far from being checked, made rapid progress, and towards the end of August she was taken back to Paris, where all the resources of the physicians' science were brought to bear upon her case. The Duchesse de Doudeauville installed herself in her beloved daughter's room, and there, for nearly three months, she passed every day, and many a night, watching every breath and heart-beat, and discerning in every feature the progress of a malady of whose gravity she had had an immediate presentiment. She clung desperately to the least gleam of hope; but Almighty God grants long seasons of suffering to those whom He has chosen to glorify Him specially. He adds fresh trials to the sacrifices that are imposed upon them by the everyday duties of their lives; He gives them to drink of the waters of tribulation, and that which is an awakening to the strayed or slumbering soul, is a recompense for the faithful one who has become the friend, the spouse of her Divine Lord, and to whom the Saviour says, as He said to His privileged disciples, "Can you drink of My chalice?"

A letter written by the Abbé Legris-Duval, a truly precious and edifying document, enables us to follow the mother and the daughter through the closing hours of that supreme struggle, in which each rivalled the other in faith, generosity, self-abnegation, and submission.

Madame de Doudeauville, who had never lost her self-command, though she had been alarmed from the first, perceiving that there was now imminent danger, wished for the assistance of one of God's ministers to aid her in sustaining, consoling, and, should it prove necessary, in preparing the beloved child of her heart to part with all she held dear. It was easy to fulfil her desire; at her fireside there was always a place for the priest—the family friend. He came, therefore, as a friend, to talk a little with the invalid, to tell her of the many graces attached to her sufferings, and the merit which she might acquire. His strength-giving words were welcome to one who had been accustomed from her childhood to read in the volume of the Divine will.

"By loving my mother," said Madame de Rastignac, "I have learned to love virtue. I have always thought that I have heard the voice of God when she was speaking, and that in obeying her I was doing His will."

In the early stage of her illness the Marquise suffered from vague and distressing presentiments, and once, in a paroxysm of that kind, she called on God to help her; after which she turned to her mother and said, "Stay with me; I have never been afaid of anything when near you." Then, under the safeguard of her mother's presence, she fell into a quiet sleep. It was natural that so ardent and trustful a spirit should shake off the first impression of fear; and the invalid did so. She was full of hope of a complete and speedy recovery; but this did not last long; first doubt and then dread again took possession of her. She studiously concealed her state of mind from her father, mother, and husband, but she sometimes revealed it to others. One day, when she was feeling more ill than usual, she said—

"I am resigned to all that God wills, but I acknowledge that it would cost me dear to quit my life in this world."

"That is perfectly natural," replied the person to whom she spoke, "at twenty-one, and with all the advantages which make you sure of happiness."

"No, no," she said laughing; "I don't mean that; those are not the bonds which hold me; you do not understand me."

"But you are a wife and mother."

"Ah! I feel that more strongly than ever; and I am a daughter!"

The last words were spoken in a heart-rending accent of grief and tenderness.

True to the unselfishness which had made it her chief joy in childhood to relieve the wants of the poor, the greatest pleasure of her youth to give to others, provided that the secret of her lavish alms were not divulged; the sweet young creature who had always been devoted to her relatives, her friends, and her servants, was wholly engrossed by consideration for others to the end. Six weeks before her death, and when she was in acute pain, she insisted on writing with her own hand to her husband, who was detained at a distance by important business, because she feared that he might be rendered uneasy by receiving a communication in a strange handwriting.

At length her state became such that she could neither remain still in any one position, nor make a movement without acute pain; but her desire to practise patience, and her fear of causing distress to those who were with her, checked every complaint, and stifled every sigh. Sometimes the sudden severity of pain would wring a groan from her, and then she would immediately try to lessen the impression produced by the sound, by smiling at her mother and her attendants, and saying a cheering word to them.

Every one who approached her received some mark of her kindness; her servants never rendered her the smallest service without being thanked with the utmost sweetness. She endeavoured to divert her father from his alarm about her by talking of everything in which he was interested, and when her husband returned she had many long interviews with him. The Marquis and his young dying wife talked of their future, and especially of the plan they had formed for their mutual sanctification.

Every day the invalid asked her mother to read a chapter of the Gospels to her; and she would make her own comments upon it. After her mother had finished the chapter, Ernestine would take the sacred volume in her hands, and kiss it with the greatest reverence. "Why are you surprised?" she said one day to a person who showed some wonder at this; "is it not the Word of God?"

On the 30th October, M. Levis, curé of the Abbaye-Saint-Germain, not considering her sufficiently ill to receive the Holy Viaticum, administered the Holy Communion to her at midnight. On the following day a decided improvement in the state of the invalid bore witness to her happiness. She was filled with joy.

"How good our Blessed Lord is!" said she; "could we ever, ever love Him enough? How He repays all our sacrifices! Is there one which I would wish to refuse Him! How much He has done for the world! Let Him dispose of me as He wills, it must always be, I know, for my good."

She attained even to the love of her sufferings. " I should be sorry to suffer less," she said repeatedly ; "Jesus Christ endured much more." And then she made it a law to herself that she would accept everything that was brought to her, notwithstanding any repugnance she might feel, in remembrance of the vinegar and gall that were offered to her Saviour.

A consultation of physicians took place early in November, and her malady was pronounced to be incurable. The Duke was present during this awful council of fate. Her mother, in mortal agony of suspense, awaited the decision by the bedside of the patient. No one came to tell her what the physicians had said ; but the silence revealed the truth to her. She also kept silence; she asked no question; but when the doctors had left the house, she sought the foot of the altar, her customary refuge. There she found her husband on his knees, and read in his tear-swollen eyes the doom that had just been pronounced upon them both. Together they offered up their sacrifice; and then, calling upon the Mother of Sorrows to aid her, the Duchess returned to her child with an aspect of perfect tranquillity. The patient, who knew that the question of her own fate had just been decided, respected her mother's silence, and did not ask a single question. When another person tried to find out what she knew, or thought, she replied simply, "I rest in the hands of Providence, as in those of my mother."

Notwithstanding the clear comprehension of her state which Madame de Rastignac evinced at intervals, she sometimes hoped, and even believed, that she should recover. Such self-delusion is a frequent accompaniment of maladies of this nature, and God permitted these alternations of hope and fear in order that the dying woman might win the reward of sacrifice, and yet that she might not be constantly oppressed by a weight too crushing for her feebleness. At length her confessor, M. Levis, warned her that the end was approaching. She seemed surprised by the intelligence, but her first thought, then, as always, was for her mother. She dreaded lest the administration of the last sacraments to herself should be a mortal blow to that beloved mother, and, fearing to allow any one else to wound the heart whose tenderness she knew so well, she resolved that from her own lips the Duchess should receive the awful warning that her hour was drawing nigh.

Think of this young woman — not twenty-one—before whom the gates of the tomb were opening, and who was hardly able to speak, setting herself to the task of inspiring her own mother with courage to see her die! After her confessor had left her, the Marquise called her mother to her and said, "M. Levis has proposed that I should receive the sacraments in a few days, do you not think it would be very edifying? Extreme unction never does any harm."

With a calm face and tearless eyes, but a breaking heart, the Duchess made answer in words full of all that maternal love and profound piety could inspire at such a moment. The patient, relieved from her great dread, allowed herself to speak out of the fulness of her heart.

"I did not think I was really so ill," she said, "but the veil is torn away now; I know that I must die; the news knocked me up; so I wanted to recover myself with you."

Listen to the answer! It is worthy of the Mother of the Maccabees.

"My daughter, if in your heart God sees the submission of Isaac, and in mine the faith of Abraham, perhaps He will arrest the sword. But let us remember Jesus Christ, His obedience, His self-devotion!"

"O mother! mother!... My only friend, you know why I must regret life.... But do not be afraid, your child will be worthy of you."

And indeed she was so, for a little while afterwards she added in a firm voice—

"Before you leave this room, we must make our sacrifice with the perfection which God demands. Mother, my sacrifice is completed.... Let us bless God, I am quite calm again. But if any of our friends should see traces of emotion about us, they might be grieved; so let us read a chapter of the 'Imitation.'"

The Duchess opened the book at random, and came upon the chapter entitled "The royal road of the Holy Cross." The mother dwelt upon these words: "In the Cross is the strength of the soul; in the Cross is the joy of the spirit, the fulfilment of virtue, the perfection of sanctity. If you carry the Cross with all your heart, it will carry you to the desired end of your journey, where you shall cease to suffer. Take up your Cross, then, and follow Jesus, and you shall attain unto eternal life."

The patient, consoled, transported with hope and joy, cried aloud, "Oh, what a treasure is the Cross! It is true, indeed, that death is gain, and suffering a real good."

Then, calling to remembrance a few

trifling matters of which she had not yet spoken to her mother, she imparted them to her, and added—" I thank God, in dying, that never in the whole course of my life have I had a single thought which I have not made known to you."

Leaving her daughter peaceful and full of trust, the poor mother, exhausted by the effort she had made, withdrew for a little while. Pale, breathless, tearless, she was heard by those around her saying to herself, over and over again, " I have no more hope; my daughter is dying!"

Madame de Rastignac, being now convinced of her danger, wished to know its precise degree. She requested that the doctor should be permitted to see her quite alone on the following day. She received him with composure and questioned him closely, observing his looks and gestures all the time. His replies conveyed to her the grim sentence that humanity would always fain mitigate. She listened to them not only without fear, but without emotion. The doctor was so deeply moved by her youth and her sad fate, and so much impressed by her courage, that he was unable to recover himself during the entire day.

Moments had now become precious; and the Marquise spoke that same day to the Abbé Legris-Duval of the happiness it would give her to receive the sacraments.

"It shall be to-morrow," she added.

"To-morrow? Your mother and your husband have been told; they would surely be desirous that these sad duties should be fulfilled as soon as possible. The waiting will be a cruel thing for them."

"You are right. I will not make them suffer. I shall have to cost them quite enough sorrow whether I will or no. It shall be this evening. I wish to spare my other relatives the pain of this spectacle; but I have entreated my mother to be present. She would regret it too much if she were kept away. Besides, I want her; she is my good angel; she is my life. I should not think I had done anything rightly without her; I owe the prolongation of my life to her care, and the salvation of my soul to her virtues."

The announcement that the solemn ceremony was about to take place, fell like a sentence of death upon the household. The old servants wept as if each of them had been losing a child; consternation was spread throughout the house; but around the bed of the dying beloved one there reigned peace and stillness. Fear and disquiet were banished from that sanctuary, in which the heroic constancy of the mother, and the gentle resignation of the daughter, triumphed. How great were both of them at that solemn moment! The mother, kneeling, forced back her tears, and permitting only the fervent aspirations of faith, in unison with the prayers of the Church, to escape from her heart, presented her daughter's hands herself to receive the sacred unction. Ernestine, peaceful and profoundly recollected, made the responses to the prayers in a firm voice.

"This is the Body of your Saviour," said the priest; "do you believe it?"

"Ah! I do indeed believe it!" she cried. Those words were uttered with so much emphasis, and such fervent love, that they who heard them repeated them with tears.

After the administration of the sacraments the Marquise rallied, the fever subsided, and she remained calm for the rest of the day, seeming to gain strength. On the following morning, however, her state again became very alarming, and all present believed that the end had come. Fixing her eyes upon her crucifix, she repeated fervently and frequently :—

"I unite my sufferings with Thine, O my Saviour. Thy merits are infinite, they will supply for my insignificance."

Towards evening she sent for the Abbé Legris-Duval.

"You must be my interpreter to my mother when I shall be no more," she said to him; "entreat her to go on living, after me, notwithstanding her grief. Tell her this was my last wish."

"You feel that you are very ill?"

"Yes, very ill."

"Poor mother! But you will pray to God to console her?"

"Ah yes! But it is you who must try to assuage her grief—it is you who must make her take care of her own life."

"Your mother still has ties and duties which she cherishes; she will take care of her health; be quite sure of that. But, if it is to be obtained from her as a grace, who can get it so well as yourself? Speak to her; we shall be certain that she will listen to us when we can remind her of what was said to her by her dying child."

"This evening I will obtain a promise from her that she will live to be a mother to my baby. I hope she will find Ernestine once more in Zénaïde. M. de Rastignac has already entreated her to adopt the child, and she has consented. How happy my daughter is! she will be brought up by my mother!"

The conversation lasted for some time longer; she concluded it by saying:—

"What will you do for me when I am dead?"

"I shall regret you, like every one who

knows you; and I will pray to God for you."

"And I shall be busy about all of you in heaven."

"You are sure of going there, then?"

"Yes, I am sure. I abandon myself entirely to God, and I am without any disquiet."

Then she fainted, and Madame de Doudeauville hastened to her. When she came to herself, she found that she was alone with her mother; and having implored her, with the most pathetic earnestness, to cherish her own life for the sake of all to whom it was so precious, she bequeathed to her the little Zénaïde. Then she begged that the Abbé Legris-Duval would come to her again, as she wished to dictate a few last wishes to him.

"Never," writes the Abbé, "had I seen her more sweet and amiable, although she was already in a sort of agony. Cold sweats, continual fainting, and hiccough, indicated the approach of the final moment." She begged him to fetch her desk, and added :—

"I am going to make my will. I am of age—I am just twenty-one."

"But, Madame, I am not a notary. I do not know how to draw out a will."

"It is only a few memoranda for my parents and for M. de Rastignac. I have never had to do anything except to let them know what it was I wished ; and then I will sign . . . if I can, for I am very weak. I should like to say that I quit this life with resignation, but deeply regretting my family. Put all that down for me."

And then, recalling all the memories, all the affections of her life, the dying woman expressed herself with such ardour, that the Abbé could hardly follow her winged words.

"Oh, what tears I am going to cost my mother—how many, and how bitter! . . . And what a sacrifice it is for me to leave her! . . . She has always made me so happy! . . . They said my education was too strict,—how little they knew my mother! . . . If I had anything to complain of, it would be too much happiness. Perhaps I was too much accustomed to fulfilling my duties for her sake. She knew how to make them all pleasant to me by the mere desire to please her. That is the truth—you are the witness of it. Promise me to tell her often that she formed all the happiness of her child; and if I have caused her any pain, pray her to pardon me." Then she spoke of her father, and lamented his misfortunes:—
"To have been banished from his family for ten years, so young as he was, and to come back to see his daughter die before his eyes! How he will grieve for

me! My brother Sosthenes will replace me with him. He will do better than I. Tell him that I rely upon his good heart, and that this thought has consoled me in dying. Repeat to M. de Rastignac that I wished to live that I might make him happy." Afterwards she spoke of her aunt, Madame de Montesquiou, whom she loved much, "because she had always told her the truth."

When the document was finished she wanted to sign it, but the Duchesse had to be called to place the desk properly for her. Her daughter hastened to prepare her to learn what was the matter in hand. "Mother," she said laughing, "I am very weak; I suppose one ought to be so when one is making one's will. My hand shakes, and I think I am losing my memory also. How ought I to spell La Rochefoucauld?" and she continued to laugh.

Supporting her daughter with one hand, and steadying the paper for her with the other, the brave mother quietly dictated each letter of the signature.

That last night was a dreadful one. No one in the house lay down. Seeing a servant enter her room during the night, the Marquise said to him—" Why have you not gone to bed; I do not wish to disturb any one."

Although her mother was now her only support, Ernestine entreated her to leave her, and rest for a while ; and when the Duchess refused, she insisted. Then the poor mother withdrew, but only to hide herself in a corner of the room, where she remained for two hours perfectly motionless, hardly daring to breathe, lest her presence should be perceived by her child. At length she did leave the room for a little while, as the Marquise had again rallied a little ; but she soon returned to the bedside, and Ernestine said to her mother, "The hour is come; shall we both have courage?"

The Abbé Legris-Duval, who entered the room at this moment, stood lost in silent admiration of the scene. The dying woman was already invested with celestial brightness and superhuman serenity; by her side stood the mother, her eyes fixed upon her daughter, calm, indeed, but a touching spectacle of maternal anguish, and a grand example of the majesty of religion and sorrow.

The Marquise addressed the priest—

"I am about to die," she said; "promise me that you will not leave me until the end?"

"Ah, Madame, I would have asked your leave to remain with you, as a great grace."

"Nor you, either, my good mother?"

A gentle pressure of the mother's arm

gave the required assurance. Then she added—

"Let us make an act of the most perfect abandonment possible. My God, I commit to Thy hands my soul and my life. I unreservedly abandon all my interests to Thy love; do with me what it pleaseth Thee. I unite my sufferings and my death with those of Jesus Christ, in whom alone I hope."

Having thus expressed her own feelings, she asked the persons now present to pray with her, and she repeated the Acts of Faith, Hope, and Charity, so fervently that she seemed to be already in the sensible presence of her God. While the other witnesses of her last moments retired to give free vent to their tears, her mother, never losing her self-command, remained close to her, uniting herself with her in the Act of Sacrifice, making her reiterate it.

All the household being assembled for the Prayers for the Agonizing, the dying daughter turned to her father, and rallying all her strength asked him, in a loud, clear voice, to give her his last blessing.

"The Duke rushed to her, embraced her, and blessed her. "Father," she said, "be calm with me; I feel too keenly the sacrifices which I have to make."

Her mother, kneeling beside her, betrayed herself this time; her tears flowed. "Keep up your courage," said Ernestine; "we need it to the end." It was then the turn of her husband and her brother, and each received her last farewell, which, indeed, was but a tryst in heaven. So joyful, so intense was hope within her, that it already transported her to the limits of her exile. "Shall I soon be in heaven? Is life nearly ended? When shall I see my God?" Thus she spoke for a while, but then, checking herself, she added, "Let us not yield to impatience; that would be giving place to temptation." With the utmost simplicity she confided her most trivial imperfections to the minister of God, and when she could hardly make herself heard, her mother patiently interpreted her confessions.

In the morning, during the mass which was offered for her, she renewed her Act of Sacrifice. Her sufferings were very great. "This is my purgatory," said she joyfully, with her eyes fixed on the crucifix and on an image of the Blessed Virgin, which she kissed by turns, repeating the sweet names of Jesus and Mary. Her last words were for her God, and for her who had taught her to love Him. Feeling her power of speech leaving her, she said in a low voice, "Mother, forgive me, and bless your daughter."

Although she had received the Holy Viaticum three days previously, M. Levis, who considered that such faith and generosity authorised a dispensation, proposed that she should again receive the Holy Communion. "It is all that I desire," said she joyfully. Time pressed, all possible haste was made. For a moment her eyelids drooped, and she seemed to lose the use of her senses; but hardly was she in the presence of Him who has said, "I am the Resurrection and the Life," than her eyes opened, and she was conscious of her happiness. She had been afraid that she would not be able to swallow the sacred Host, and with a childlike gesture, and in a tone of delight, she exclaimed, "Mother! I have been able to receive." These were her last words. On the instant she lost consciousness, but there was no agitation, no struggle; her state was more like that of a soul wrapt in blessed contemplation than the final failing of nature.

While the weeping beholders were asking themselves whether she was in heaven or on earth, the dying Christian bent her head gently towards her mother, and the angelic spirit passed so tranquilly that only M. Lévis perceived the moment of its departure.

The Duchess, on her knees, and motionless, was watching for another breath, another movement. She said, "Ernestine?"

No one ventured to speak. Then M. Lévis, without a word, drew the crucifix from the hands of the daughter, and placed them in those of the mother. What a sublime, what an agonising sight was that mother to look upon! She uttered not a cry, not a murmur, but the torrent of her long-restrained tears gushed forth and bathed the cross, which she

R

kissed, and held fast to her lips, as if she too would fain have breathed her last sigh upon it.

After a short silence M. de Doudeauville begged his wife to withdraw.

"I will do whatever you wish," was her answer, " though I am better here than anywhere else." A few minutes more elapsed, and then the Duke again entreated her to go downstairs with him. She rose, advanced to the bed, fell on her knees, uttered a short prayer, once more embraced the beloved form, and without a cry or a gesture, she quitted her child for ever.

The Duchess went down to her own room, and received all the family with the most pathetic kindness; but her strength was spent, the limits of her endurance were overpast. After a short time she fainted, and on recovering from the swoon, she fell into a sort of delirium. On the subsidence of the raving she suffered for some time from complete prostration; but under all circumstances, when her grief was keenest, and her desolation deepest, she felt and expressed perfect resignation.

CHAPTER VII.

QUIET LIFE.

THERE are times when the closing in of the day towards evening inspires us with an irresistible sadness, and a similar sense of depression falls upon the human being who, having passed the meridian of life and entered upon its decline, appraises the value of all things here below by the standard of his own experience. Let us not lament that it is so, for that is the moment at which a rich and abundant spiritual harvest begins to ripen for him. The autumn has not, indeed, the freshness and the perfume of the spring, but its gifts are more useful and more precious.

The second portion of the life of the Duchesse de Doudeauville had no such striking features as the first, but it was none the less rich in marvels of grace and sanctity. Her mission was unchanged; the past had given her an irresistible influence over all who belonged to her; by constant striving to annihilate self, by devotion as constant to the happiness of all around her, she had established her empire over those hearts which yielded gladly to an ascendancy exercised with so much loving mildness and humility. The very sight of the Duchess recalled the canticle of her whom she strove to imitate : " My soul doth magnify the Lord! He hath regarded the humility of His handmaid."

The accents of thanksgiving were, indeed, those in which she habitually spoke, even after the greatest sacrifices had been demanded of her, and it seems as though the breath of vanity was never permitted to reach her. The blow that had fallen upon her left profound and lasting sadness in her heart; the image of her daughter, which was always before her eyes, led her still more frequently to the foot of the cross. This truly afflicted mother sought no diversion from her grief; she only strove to unite it with that which had been endured on Calvary.

Ever since the Revolution it had been one of the most fervent desires of the pious Duchess to contribute to the full extent of her means to the raising up of the overthrown altar, the restoration of churches and other consecrated buildings to their original purpose, and that of parishes to their lawful pastors. When the country was tranquil, and affairs wore a somewhat settled aspect, she returned to the favourite estate, whose name, Montmirail, she had borne in her girlhood, having made the necessary application to the authorities; she spared no efforts or sacrifices in order to procure a faithful priest for the church of Montmirail, in the place of the person who had usurped the functions of parish priest there.

The clergy-house, which had been used as a station for gendarmerie for several years, was, owing to her exertions and especially to her liberality, given up to the use of the new curé, and suitably prepared for his accommodation. While she was negotiating these important affairs, but before she had brought them to a satisfactory conclusion, the Duchess made a considerable purchase. There existed at Montléan, a suburb of Montmirail, the remains of an ancient Benedictine Priory, and Madame de Doudeauville ardently desiring to save the church from complete destruction, to have a safe place in which the Catholic worship might be celebrated, and to offer a reparation to our Divine Lord for the outrages that had been committed during the Revolution, purchased the Priory. She was especially induced to do so by the pitiable condition to which the small hospital, founded by the blessed Jean de Montmirail,` had been reduced. The poor patients were wretchedly lodged in an inconvenient tenement, and handed over to mere mercenary care, without any real relief for either body or mind being afforded them. The Duchess conceived the idea of transporting this hospital to the chief portion of the building at Montléan.

In the old times of the Gondi de Retz family, the Château de Montmirail had been honoured by the presence of Saint Vincent de Paul, who was tutor to the famous cardinal; and the illustrious founder of Saint-Lazare and of the Sisters of

Charity had not forgotten the little town of La Brie among the pious establishments he had projected at that epoch. The Duchess, faithfully preserving these sacred and honourable memories, confided the new hospital to the zealous and intelligent care of the Sisters of Charity. She added to the hospital a small free school, and a work school for poor orphans; but it was not without great difficulty that she succeeded in carrying out her pious projects.

While she was labouring in this cause with the utmost zeal it pleased Almighty God to afflict her in the most grievous manner, by recalling her beloved daughter to Himself. This sad event led her to reserve for herself that portion of the church which, during several centuries, had been a place of pilgrimage to the Blessed Virgin. She resolved to restore it, to consecrate it to the Cross, and to have a vault made underneath it, in which her Ernestine should be laid. She desired to have her child near her, to be able to hasten her happiness by praying upon her grave, to find there her inspiration to good works, to draw from it the blessed hope of reunion with her now-hidden treasure, and courage to be faithful to all the demands of grace.

While the Duchess was engaged in carrying out this plan, a fresh grief fell upon her. She was detained in Paris by some urgent business, although she was especially anxious to get back to Montmirail, where she had left her mother-in-law, who was indisposed. At the earliest possible moment she started for the château with her husband. On the road an accident happened to the carriage, and the Duchess believed for a few moments that her son had been crushed under the wheels. She received so severe a shock that her health was much impaired by it for a long time afterwards. This was but the beginning of the troubles of that sad journey. As the noble travellers drew near the house, the faces of the persons whom they met wore embarrassed looks, and on their arrival at the château the Duke and Duchess were alarmed by the hesitation of the servants' replies to their anxious questions. The presentiments which they both felt were only too well founded: the Vicomtesse de la Rochefoucauld had expired calmly a few hours previously while sitting in her arm-chair. Neither she nor any one about her could have foreseen that the end of her life was near. A heart which has been already wounded feels a new grief very keenly; the Duchess and her husband mourned deeply for the true mother they had lost. The great sorrows which they had borne together had united the hearts of the Vicomtesse and her daughter-in-law very closely. In the midst of their grief, the mourners acknowledged the great, the only consolation, that of knowing that in this case death, though " sudden," had not been " unprovided." Under the influence and in the society of her daughter-in-law Madame de la Rochefoucauld had become as pious as by nature she had always been amiable.

The project of making Montléan a place of burial was not realised without great difficulty. Madame de Doudeauville met with opposition in quarters whence she had least reason to expect it; but she persevered in her enterprise with equal firmness and moderation, and at length she overcame every obstacle.

On the 14th September 1804, the chapel at Montléan was solemnly opened.

The Abbé Legris-Duval announced, in an eloquent discourse, that permission had been granted by the Sovereign Pontiff, for the dedication of the Altar to the Cross, and the celebration of the Feasts of the Finding and the Elevation of the Holy Cross, with their octaves according to the rubrics.

Two days later the remains of Madame de Rastignac were deposited in the vault at Montléan, together with those of the Vicomtesse de la Rochefoucauld, and the heart of the Maréchal d'Estrées.

M. de Doudeauville was travelling in Italy with his son and the Marquis de Rastignac, when the removal of his daughter's remains from Paris to Montléan took place. The Duchess, who had made all the arrangements for the re-interment, wrote to him on the occasion in the following touching words:—

"The removal of our beloved daughter

is taking place to-day. Forgive me if I pain you by the details I am about to give you; but my own poor heart tells me what interest they will have for you.

I had not ventured to give expression to the idea that engrossed me, thinking it must be impossible; I did, however, ask Arnolet, whose attachment to us made him desire to be one of the spectators, to ascertain the state in which she was. His reply, which was formed upon the information he had obtained, convinced me that after a year nothing of what once was our child could remain. But, to the great astonishment of all, they found her precisely as she was at the moment of her death, not the slightest sign of the corruption of the grave had passed upon her. Arnolet recognised her perfectly, and that this was the case. They uncovered her face only, but as she was removed with perfect ease from the coffin in which she lay and placed in another, it is plain that her body was in a similar state of preservation. Why could I not have seen her once more! They tell me that an expression of beatitude was on her face. If I could have seen that, and could now cherish it with the remembrance of the heroism of her last moments, it might give me the certainty of her present happiness, and it seems to me I should be less wretched. All will soon be completed, and then I shall have this precious charge in my possession, and you after me, and our son after us both. May we all meet again in heaven!"

The new church somewhat resembled a tomb in its form and the manner in which it was lighted, also in its stillness and solitude. On the left of the nave was a chapel, dedicated to Our Lady of Pity. In the centre of the sanctuary stood the altar, which was reached by five steps, and surrounded by funereal emblems; at the back a heap of rough stones, covered with moss, formed a little mound, supporting a simple cross, formed of a pine-trunk with the bark on. This cross, standing back in the darkness, was dimly lighted by a lamp concealed by the altar. The vault was constructed underneath the sanctuary.

The Duchess came frequently to the foot of this cross, there to renew before the Lord the sacrifice of all that was dearest to her in the world, and to gain strength for her soul by contemplating the sufferings and the humiliation of the Sacred Heart of Jesus.

The care she bestowed on everything connected with the services of the church did not hinder her from exercising the utmost diligence, discretion, and wisdom in the direction of her household and the affairs of her family; nor did her growing attraction towards the sorrowful mysteries produce any alteration in the sweet cheerfulness of her demeanour, or in the kindliness of her relations with all her relatives, friends, and dependants. Devoted, generous, and vigilant in all things, she perfectly fulfilled her duties as a wife and mother, as the mistress of a great house, and a lady of rank and importance in the country; her eyes were on all things; her heart went out to all her people; no passion ever troubled it. She was actuated by only one desire, that of doing good. To relieve, to cure, to console, to preserve, and to edify,—such were the objects of her thoughts and the motives of her actions. The grace of God had so deeply penetrated her soul that she no longer knew any distinction between the express commandment and that which is of counsel only; the most perfect had become an imperious necessity to her.

Her little grand-daughter, Zénaïde, had become doubly dear to the Duchess since the tie of nature had been rendered additionally sacred by the solemn bequest of her dying daughter. Recommencing the task she had so admirably fulfilled in the early days of her own married life, she watched over the motherless little girl with the tenderest solicitude, and, fearing lest the inevitable air of mourning that surrounded her first years should sadden a period of life which ought to be full of gaiety and animation, she gave Zénaïde a companion for her hours of study and recreation. Thérèse Pérardel* was of the same age as Zénaïde, she was brought up with her, and became

* See Note.

a friend of both the grandmother and the grand-daughter, on whose discretion and devotion they could entirely rely, in whom they placed absolute confidence, and who never left them.

It is very difficult to hold all the powers of the mind in perfect equilibrium, so that the fulfilment of one duty shall never interfere with the fulfilment of another, nor one strong affection become exclusive; this difficulty was, however, surmounted by the saintly Duchesse de Doudeauville. The Duke carefully preserved the letters written to him by his wife during his travels, after the death of their daughter. This correspondence sets her before us as the perfect example of a wife entirely and intelligently devoted to her duty. She consults her husband on every occasion, and always with the utmost deference; and when she states her own opinions, she does so with such tact and delicacy that she seems to ask advice rather than to dictate a decision.

"I hope you will not disapprove of my little excursion," she writes, "because in everything I do I always endeavour to divine your wishes."

While she was scrupulously exact in her observance of the laws of the Church, she knew how to combine the respect due to them with the necessary care of her husband's health. We find her writing to him as follows:—

"One respect in which I blame you absolutely is your intention of observing the fast while you are drinking the waters. I beg you to consult the doctor on this point, and do what he advises. You have manifested the firmness of your faith by strictly observing the laws of abstinence hitherto; and I am convinced that you would do yourself a real injury by continuing to observe them. I do not know whether my letter will reach you, but I do know that I am in constant anxiety about your health; and that the certainty I feel of having been once deceived about it is not reassuring for either the present or the future, and justifies the uneasiness from which I am never for a moment free. I am vexed with my son about this, a little vexed with his wife also, and indeed with everybody, except the doctor who cured you."

These letters, and others like them, are delightful to read, so exquisitely are ardent piety and the tenderest affection blended in them:

"How happy you are to have been at Annecy! I would give up all the rest of your travels for that one expedition, but not the pleasure which I should have had in making it with you. What enchanting moments I have passed at the tomb of your favourite saint! How much his intercession did towards restoring me to peace of mind, and dispersing the mephitic vapours in which my sojourn at Genoa had shrouded me! What blessed visits to the poor were those which I made there! What lessons I learned, what examples of the Christian virtues I beheld! God permitted it to be so, and the remembrance will be ever dear to me. The thought of it causes me strong emotion, for even the aching of my poor heart, torn with grief as it is, cannot hinder my soul from rejoicing over all that binds it to its God. Herein consists the happiness of the Christian! Taste of that happiness, my dear husband; may all whom we love partake of it likewise, and may we one day drink deep draughts from the spring of never ending joy in heaven."

The Duc de Doudeauville insisted that his wife, who had, by her great courage, and at the peril of her life, preserved all the property of the family in safety during the Revolution, should retain the entire management of it. She obeyed him in this; but while she had the trouble and responsibility of their large fortune, she took care that the chief portion of the enjoyment, and all the honour of it, should be his. She detailed minutely to him every change she proposed to make, every measure which she regarded as advisable; she awaited his decisions; she wished all orders to emanate from him; and if any discussion ever arose between them, it was because each wished to yield the right of settling the question to the other.

The Duchess, who was in every sense a superior woman, was endowed with a great faculty for order and administration. She entered into the smallest details, made up her accounts herself, and transacted all the business of a great landowner with the farmers. She was not to be imposed upon by anybody. Her constant and comprehensive vigilance was dictated as much by charity as by her sense of right; she regarded herself merely as the steward of the goods of her children and the poor. While she was careful to prevent dishonesty or waste, and even to suppress all unnecessary expenditure, she maintained her household on a footing that was perfectly suitable to her rank; and when an occasion arose for her to aid, or even to oblige others, she was nobly open-handed. In her those precious qualities, perfect order and inexhaustible generosity, were united; there is hardly a rarer combination in the human character. Her susceptibility and delicacy of feeling in money matters were extreme; she was always inclined to pronounce judgment against herself in any doubtful question ; and when such occasions arose, she would say to her men of business: "I beg of you, gentlemen, not to send me to purgatory for the sake of money."

The following letter reveals the clear-mindedness and accurate judgment of one who, undazzled by wealth, wishes to regulate expenses exactly by the means at her disposal, and shews us with what tact, grace, and kindness she could make an important sacrifice :—

"You will never find me reluctant, when it is a question of giving pleasure to others, above all, to friends of yours; besides, you are perfectly at liberty to use your fortune as you choose; and I shall either applaud whatever you do, or keep silence on the subject; but I must tell you frankly that, though we are rich people, we have not much to spare. If we do not restrict our generosity and curtail our expenses, we shall either leave debts behind us, or we shall exhaust our capital, which comes to the same thing. Neither of these results would accord with our principles, or with our attachment to our children. These reflections arise from the business in which I am engaged, and the alarm with which I am inspired by the almost incalculable amount of our charges: they seem to grow heavier every day. I think it is very doubtful whether Monsieur de N—— will be able to repay the fifteen thousand francs; but I shall share the pleasure it will give you to hand the money to him."

As we follow the course of the correspondence between the Duke and Duchess, we speedily discover the secret of these heavy charges upon their resources,—it is their boundless charity. Pensions for life were settled upon numerous persons who had done them services, and on several individuals who had fallen into a state of poverty from opulence. For the latter kind of misfortune Madame de Doudeauville felt especial respect. Again, her servants formed so strictly an integral portion of her family that, once admitted to the hôtel in Paris or the château at Montmirail, they remained there all the rest of their lives. Their old age was tenderly cheered and cared for, and they were sedulously tended in their illnesses or infirmities.

Faith, charity, and consideration have seldom found simpler or more complete expression than in the few following lines addressed by the pious Duchess to her husband:—

"Your man from Verneuil has arrived. He is a very interesting person, and he is very happy about entering your service. But you had not told me that his wife was an invalid; so that, when they made their appearance, I was quite taken aback on beholding a poor sufferer, just about to be tapped for dropsy. But I have returned thanks to Almighty God, saying to myself that by this sign we are to recognise that they were destined for us."

Such generous feelings as these could hardly fail to secure the gratitude and fidelity of their objects, and indeed it was so. That true and oft-repeated saying, " Good masters make good servants," was perhaps never more fully borne out than at the Château de Montmirail.

The Duc de Doudeauville gives an affecting description of the courageous fidelity exhibited by his servants, when, during the terrible invasion of 1814, the Château de Montmirail was threatened with destruction, and he ascribes its preservation entirely to their devotion. He tells the story as follows:—

"That our Château de Montmirail is still standing, while the greater number of the houses in the neighbourhood have been pillaged and laid waste, is due to the courage of our own people. Being detained in Paris ourselves, we were obliged to depend entirely upon them for the defence of our interests; the chief responsibility resting upon an old servant of my own family, who had come to us as housekeeper. Her name was Langlois. For nearly two months she never went to bed, remaining on the watch all night; and notwithstanding her sixty years, she was obliged to confront the succession of inimical visitors who disturbed the château every day. On one occasion her courage was severely tested. Some Cossacks had been killed in passing through Montmirail, and their regiment arrived the following day, bent on burning down the village. After much negotiation and supplication, a commutation of punishment was obtained; six hours' pillage of Montmirail, and two hours' pillage of the château, were considered a sufficient expiation of the bloodshed. The inhabitants had all fled into the woods. Our old housekeeper only stood bravely to her post; and presenting herself boldly before the forty Cossacks who had come to execute the orders of their commandant, she asked them what they had come for?

"'Pillage!' they replied, with Spartan brevity.

"'Very well; I will open the doors, and show you the way,' she rejoined, with quiet self-possession. This she did, thus preventing violence and disorder.

"During the two hours allowed for the work, our brave servant remained with the soldiers, keeping them quiet, preventing wanton destruction of our property, and even hindering them from carrying off the most precious articles. Her admirable conduct, her rare courage, made a great impression on the men; and eight years afterwards, one of the royal princes of Prussia asked a relative of mine at St. Petersburg whether the good old lady, who had kept the Cossacks within bounds, was still living? She could not, however, succeed in saving our poor merinos sheep from the spoilers, although she had taken such clever measures for their defence that the soldiers called her General Langlois.

"The Cossacks, however, invented a novel method of fishing, which afforded them a great deal of amusement. They stripped some tiles off the floor of the lofts over the sheepfold, and through the holes they let down lassoes, with which they caught the sheep, declaring their 'take' to be capital fish. The game cost us two hundred prime merinos; but the invention made us laugh, in spite of its telling so heavily against ourselves.

"On one occasion, Napoleon breakfasted at our château; on another he slept there. The second visit was near costing us dear. Finding his room too small for his huge maps, he insisted on having what he called the partition thrown down; but our good Langlois resisted him as sturdily as she resisted everybody else in our interests; and the partition, which was nothing less than a stone wall three feet thick, was saved.

"While the Cossacks were seizing upon all whom they met, and forcing them to act as guides,—a service in which numbers died under the blows of their taskmasters, or from exhaustion,—my poor old steward, Gallet, who was then seventy years old, went about our deserted farms, labouring to repair the devastation to which they had been subjected.

"As for my valet, Raphaël, the faithful companion of my long exile, he gave me, in those dark days, ever new proofs of his devotion to our service. In a letter, which by a happy chance reached me, he wrote: 'They are fighting in the village, they are fighting in the courtyard of your château; the balls are striking the room in which I am writing; I know not what will be our fate; but rest assured that to the last moment we shall prove ourselves worthy of our good master and mistress. I only commend my poor children to you.

"We sent word to them, by various means, to leave the place, to abandon everything; assuring them that we much preferred the loss of all we possessed to the knowledge that they were exposed to such danger, and to leaving them in such scenes of tribulation. All our entreaties were vain, not one of them would desert his post; and the servants who were with us in Paris urgently demanded our permission to join their comrades in their efforts to save our property. We were deeply touched by these proofs of the attachment of our people, and amply compensated by them for all our losses."

The Duchess looked upon domestic vexations both great and small, which, by their demand on the exercise of charity silently increase the number of humble and stable virtues, as a distinct grace.

It was her custom to reprove her dependants with gentle firmness, but she selected the time and the manner of her reproofs with unfailing discernment; and she bore the oddities of all those who surrounded her, their natural imperfections, even the defects that she recognised as incorrigible, with immovable patience. She never complained of the conduct of any one towards herself; and, by her example as well as by her advice, she induced others to extend to their fellows that mutual support which is indispensable to unity of heart and concord of life. The very sight of the Duchess was enough to dispel a cloud between any two persons, the serenity in her face shed something of its heavenly peace on all who approached her. They felt that she lived continually in the presence of her God; but her inexhaustible kindness did not prevent her from being dignified and imposing, especially when she intended to administer a lesson.

In spite of the general order by which all priests who had taken the revolutionary oath were excluded from her house, one of these persons contrived to make his way into the presence of the Duchesse de Doudeauville. He found her alone, in her salon, and seated. She did not rise to receive him, nor did she invite him to take a chair, but he, with insolent freedom, seated himself, unasked. The Duchess immediately rose, and listened, standing, to what he had to say, preserving an air of cold and stately gravity. The unhappy man, thoroughly disconcerted by her attitude, which was more expressive than a long speech, got out of the room as quickly as he could. While the intrusion of this person lasted, the Duchess never appeared at any of the services in the parish church, but had mass said for her, in her private gallery, by a faithful priest.

She was careful to give scandal to none, according to the counsel of the apostle, which bids us be considerate of the weak brethren. While she was engaged in making vestments and ornaments for the church, she frequently employed her leisure moments on Sundays in examining the work she had done during the past week, and comparing it with the design, which was drawn by herself.* One Sunday, while she was sitting at her embroidery frame, surrounded with pencils and papers, the wife of one of the farmers on the estate came to see her, and was ushered into the *salon*. The Duchess, fearing that the sight of her working materials might give scandal to the good woman, explained, after they had discussed her visitor's affairs, that the work on which she was engaged was not a servile occupation, and therefore not interdicted by the law of God; but she speedily perceived that she was not, and never would be, understood. Each explanation which she attempted to make, was met by the good woman with the same unvarying answer: "Yes, Madame, I understand

* See Note.

very well; each one works after his own fashion."

From that day the Duchess laid aside her pencils, never more to use them on Sundays or holy days.

It was not only occasionally, or when the fancy took her, that the Duchess applied herself to needlework. Realising in every respect King Solomon's ideal of the "valiant woman," she was an adept in the use of the needle, and she never lost a moment of time. She was zealous in the interests of the poor and of the churches. Visitors admitted to intimacy with her invariably found her occupied, and her needlework was of great service in supplying her with an excuse for withdrawing from general conversation when she thought fit to do so. She would sometimes be observed to lose herself in the intricacies of her tapestry pattern, and then to reappear all of a sudden and lead those who had strayed from the path of charity back into it, gently and without rebuke. On such occasions her first words would be received with general smiles; every one was aware of her little manœuvre, her reputation was an established one in all similar respects.

The unremitting industry of the Duchess was a favourite theme with her husband, who addressed some verses to her on this quality. The composition is a clever and humorous one, and is a proof of the esteem and veneration in which he held her.* The Duc de Doudeauville had a taste for poetry, he also wrote verses with ease and elegance; and as he believed that his wife was the one woman "beyond compare" in all the world, he took advantage of every imaginable opportunity to express his sentiments in his

---

* As the Duke's verses are a continuous play upon the French word *point* (stitch), it is not possible to translate them. They will be found at the end of the volume.

favourite fashion. Each year, in advance of Saint Augustine's day, he wrote a number of verses appropriate to the occasion, and distributed them to all around him, so that each had a little congratulatory compliment ready to offer to the Duchess on the feast of her patron saint. Madame de Doudeauville accepted these demonstrations very graciously, although they were not naturally to her taste; but one year the number of compositions was so great, that from morning until night she was condemned to hear her own praises sung, or declaimed, by every one who came near her. This was such a painful St. Augustine's day to her that she begged her husband to spare her a penance of the same kind in future, and from that time forth he contented himself with writing verses that her grandchildren (who were becoming numerous as she advanced in years), might repeat to her on the auspicious occasion. One real pleasure the annual festivities brought to the pious Duchess; this was the entertainment given to the poor of the district. Her entire happiness consisted in promoting that of others; what her own feelings were we may trace in the following extract from one of her letters to her husband:—

"I must acknowledge," she writes, "that as I am thoroughly settled here I should be very sorry to go elsewhere. The same reasons which have attached me to this dwelling for years still exist, and will continue to bind me to it until my last sigh; but they are all concentrated in one dark and narrow spot. As for the remainder of the place, it has become for me what, I believe, all places under the sun would be; that is, real and lifelike only according to the more or less of happiness which I can see those whom I love enjoying in it, for it is only my heart which is not dead in me. Let me say so once for all, and return to it no more; I would rather not think aloud on this point."

What that "dark and narrow spot" was, we know. As the Duchess could not resort to it so constantly as she desired, she had a small portion of the garden reserved for her own exclusive use; a simple and solemn little hermitage whither she loved to retire. The inhabitants of Montmirail were in the constant habit of walking in the magnificently-wooded park, of which the Duchess generously made them all free; but it was understood that no one was to go beyond a certain green boundary line that marked the retreat of the saintly Duchess. There, seated on the trunk of a fallen tree, she watched the walls of Montléan rising from their ruins; there, while a dwelling for our Divine Lord in the Eucharist, and a resting-place for her beloved daughter, were in course of preparation, she meditated long upon the instability of the things of this world. Her meditations, while they strengthened her longing to reach the end of her exile, made her desire all the more ardently the perfect accomplishment of the Divine Will.

We must not, however, allow it to be supposed that the dwellers in the château, or the guests of the Duchess, had to suffer from her taste for solitude. No one did the honours of a great house, or fulfilled the duties of a kindly hospitality, better than Madame de Doudeauville; in every sense one breathed a beneficent air in her domain of Montmirail. Although the presence of the noble and pious lady of the house brought edification with it; although those who talked with her felt that they were drawn nearer to God, there were no tiresome homilies or pompous exhortations to be feared from her; a passing word, a gleam from the fire in her heart, would give the observer a glimpse of the ardour of her faith ; but she never preached. There was in her such intense compassion for every kind of suffering that, without any direct advance from her, those who were with her felt impelled to disclose the secrets of their soul, the burthen of their hearts to her. Then she would speak words which the hearers could never forget, and which would bring them back again and again to her as to a life-giving spring. The young Vicomtesse de la Rochefoucauld, in particular, enjoyed and profited by the society of her mother-in-law. In 1806, the Vicomte Sosthenes had married the only daughter of Mathieu, Duc de Montmorency. M. de Doudeauville says of the Vicomtesse: "She was adorned even more richly by her gentle piety than by the charms of her person."

Happy was it for the young wife, married at sixteen, and of a naturally timid disposition, to have been placed under the wise and gentle direction of such a mother-in-law. She concealed nothing from that true and trusted friend; but imparted her inmost thoughts and griefs to her with absolute confidence. The Duchess loved, esteemed, and sustained her; and took the greatest pleasure in sounding her praises. She needed only to say to her: " My daughter, this is a duty!" and there were no more objections, all reluctance was conquered, and the young Vicomtesse would eagerly set about doing the things she most disliked.

A close friendship subsisted between the Duc de Doudeauville and the Duc de Montmorency, and when, in 1814, the latter was banished from Paris for the offence to the Emperor Napoleon of having visited Madame de Staël, who had saved his life, he took up his abode with his friend at the Château de Montmirail, where he passed his three years of exile very pleasantly. Madame de Montesquiou, who was in favour with Napoleon, had obtained this modification of the proscription in his favour. She was at that time governess to the King of Rome, and, her brother-in-law tells us, " much against her own will." It was Madame de Doudeauville whom the Emperor had in the first instance selected to bring up his son, but, having prudently made soundings in that direction, he soon saw that he must not expose himself to a refusal, and he then made choice of Madame de Montesquiou. In the Memoirs of M. de Doudeauville, we find an anecdote which illustrates the uprightness and firmness of this lady, who was worthy to be the sister of the Duchess.

" The Comtesse of Montesquiou," writes the Duke, " was held in high esteem and consideration by the Chief of the State; but she never made any use of her favour at his Court except in the interests of others, or for the pleasure of her acquaintances.

"The manner in which she attained this position was singular, and deserves to be recorded. The post had been spoken of for her, but nothing at all had been decided in respect to it. She happened to be at Trianon when Bonaparte arrived there, on one of his sudden excursions. He never had more than seven or eight people at his table; and she, not expecting to be summoned, had begged the chamberlain on duty not to forget her two dishes of fasting fare, for it was Friday. All of a sudden she was told that she was to dine with the Emperor, and she was, in fact, placed by his side at table. Much more occupied with her conscience than with the honours which had been done her, she was greatly embarrassed by perceiving that there was not a dish of which she could eat; but summoning up courage she began composedly to dine on bread and butter. Her imposing neighbour observed her, but said nothing; and the discomfort of my poor sister-in-law was augmented when she beheld the dishes that she had requested might be served for her dinner in her own apartment carried in and placed on the Imperial table. She fully expected that her haughty host would be offended by such a breach of etiquette; but nevertheless she ate what had been served for her use, quite alone; and still Napoleon looked at her, but never said a word.

"Everybody thought the Comtesse had ruined herself for ever in his estimation by this act. Two days afterwards she received her nomination as Governess to the King of Rome. The brother of the Emperor of Austria, who was also present at this dinner, had not sufficient courage to follow the example of Madame de Montesquiou. A few days afterwards he said to one of her children: 'I admired your mother, but I did not venture to imitate her, although my principles are the same as hers. She displayed such courage as made me both envious and ashamed.'

"The only person in Napoleon's court who ventured to speak boldly and frankly to him was Madame de Montesquiou. One day, when he had come with Berthier to visit the little prince, he took the child's hand in his, and said—

"'I hope that hand will learn to give a cut with a sword, some day.'

"'And I,' said the governess, 'hope that before then that hand will have learned to confer many benefits.'"

CHAPTER VIII.

NAZARETH.

When Madame de Doudeauville saw that her works of charity at Montléan were prospering in the hands of the sisters, her indefatigable zeal began to seek for a new outlet. She had reserved to herself a modest dwelling not far from the church, and having gathered together within its walls a few nuns whose convents had been dismantled in the Revolution, and their inmates dispersed, she formed a small boarding school for them, composed for the most part of children belonging to good families who had been ruined by the misfortunes of the period.

The Abbé Legris-Duval was their first

superior. He gave them, not rules, because each had her own, but certain wise principles of conduct, intended to establish union and charity among them. The new community took the name of "Dames de la Paix."

Notwithstanding the diversity of spirit which must necessarily exist among persons who severally belong to different religious orders, the house gained a good reputation, and under the direction of the excellent Abbé Legris-Duval, its pupils were trained in principles of practical piety.

The good Duchess, like Madame de Maintenon at Saint Cyr, was the heart and soul of the institution, and she impressed the simple and solid character of her own gentle and courageous virtues on the education which was given there inspiring the pupils with the spirit of order, economy, and love of study, and with the sentiment of duty. Her great desire was that the nuns should train girls to be serious and sensible women, useful and agreeable members of their respective families, capable of exercising influence and of practising self-denial in the cause of good.

The gentleness and tact of the Abbé Legris-Duval were unrivalled, and so long as he lived the community agreed together very well; but when he died the good understanding between the nuns came to an end; each endeavoured to enforce her own former rule, and the result was discord. At the entreaty of the Duchesse, M. Frayssinous in the first instance, and, after him, the Père Roger, endeavoured to pacify the Ladies of Peace. The efforts of each in his turn proved equally unsuccessful, and then both combined in offering advice to Madame de Doudeauville. They were men of great and varied experience, and they were equally struck by the wisdom and loftiness of the Duchess's views; but they were convinced that she could never attain her object while such diversity of spirit continued to exist, and they therefore advised her to forbid any additions to the number of the community, and to let it die out by degrees.

The superior, who had applied to the Duchess for permission to commence a new building, was annoyed at receiving a refusal. She made secret preparations for her departure, and removed with her little colony into another diocese. This desertion, which, however, was not to be regretted, placed the Duchess in a position of great embarrassment, a very common forerunner of actively providential aid. She might have merely removed her young *protégées* to another educational establishment and turned the house at Montléan to some other purpose, but it seemed to her that Almighty God required of her the continuation of this particular work. Her granddaughter, Mademoiselle de Rastignac, had recently become the wife of the Comte de la Rochefoucauld, and she had therefore no child to be about her in her own house. It was a great solace to her to pay frequent visits to the little schoolgirls who owed their maintenance and education to her. When she knelt at the tomb, whither she came to seek for pious inspirations, she seemed to hear herself earnestly urged to perpetuate, so far as it should be in her power, that mission to the young to which she had hitherto been so faithful.

All circumstances and events contained instruction for the meditative mind of the Duchess, and she passed on rapidly from reflection to practical action, always widening the circle of good to be done, and feeling that she was called upon to associate herself with the great movement that was manifesting itself on all sides after the long reign of evil in France. She was well aware that the reconstruction of the edifice would have to be commenced from the foundation, and she observed with great satisfaction that several religious congregations, both long established and modern, were devoting themselves to the education of young girls. On that important task the Duchess had certain ideas and thoughts of her own, the fruits of her experience.

If, as she said to her daughter, the fallen greatness, the complete overthrow of everything which had taken place before her eyes, had forced her to acknowledge that "God only is lasting!" the uncertainty of all things had also led her to recognise the necessity of strengthening the character of young girls, of teaching them, well in advance, to bear the reverses of fortune when they should come, not only in the spirit of faith, but with intelligent and practical courage. She would have had them initiated by degrees, according to their age, into the details of domestic life; so that if at any time they should find themselves obliged to wait on themselves and those belonging to them, they should not feel the necessity a hardship or a degradation, or be unequal to tasks which are sanctified by their motive and by duty, and highly praised in the Holy Scriptures.

With this object in view, Madame de Doudeauville wished to place within the reach of those families who regarded the luxury of the great world with alarm and disapprobation such educational establishments as should develop these ideas. The schools were to be conducted on a system which, while affording a complete and high-class education to the pupils, would make it a special aim to preserve them in noble and old-world simplicity, to cultivate in them industrious and notable habits; in short, to train them to be good mothers and capable housewives. In addition to these views on education, the Duchess entertained a profound appreciation of the religious life; in which she wished for spiritual perfection, and also extreme simplicity in external practices.

It will not have been forgotten that in her early girlhood, indeed while she was yet a child, she had ardently longed for the solitude of the cloister. Her earnest desire had been to give herself entirely to God. He had accepted the offering; and though He retained and fixed her in the world, contrary to all her expectations, He did not condemn the first and holy desire of His willing servant to sterility.

He predestined and prepared her, far in advance, to become the foundress of a new congregation. While that preparation was in progress; while the grace of God was causing the lovely and fragrant virtues, of which the Holy Family in the little town of Nazareth afforded the perfect example, to bud and blossom in this elect soul, His providence had exposed the Duchess to all the difficulties of life; and made her an example to the young girls whose welfare became her engrossing care, of all that they ought to be in their family life and in society.

Père Roger, who was endowed with an especial gift of discernment of the Divine inspiration, believed that it was clearly to be recognised in the project which the Duchesse de Doudeauville confided to him. He did not immediately see how it was to be carried out, but he advised her to keep up the little boarding-school, which had been abandoned by the Dames de la Paix, in its actual condition. The Duchess was called upon for an immediate sacrifice in obedience to the counsel given her by Père Roger; no less than a temporary separation between herself and Mademoiselle Thérèse, her reader and secretary, whom she had to place at the head of the school, while she awaited the further manifestation of the will of God.

The new edifice was not destined to be constructed of old materials; the energy and discernment of Père Roger speedily provided new stones for this building which was to be dedicated to the honour of God. At this stage of our narrative, it is fitting that we should make a brief allusion to the career of the holy monk whom Providence sent to the venerable founder, that he might be the soul of the work which she was contemplating.

Père Roger was born at Coutances, in

1763, and, having made his studies in Paris with remarkable steadiness and piety, he received Holy Orders in that city. He retired to Germany during the tempestuous period of the Revolution, and there some young ecclesiastics of his acquaintance induced him to enter the Society of the Fathers of the Sacred Heart, afterwards the Society of the Fathers of the Faith.

In the year 1800, his superiors sent Père Roger back to France. A vast field for the exercise of his talents and his zeal was afforded by the city of Lyons, where he established several associations, all animated by his own fervent spirit, whose members devoted themselves entirely to works of mercy, performed in humility and silence.

In 1808 a fresh political storm arose, and the pious missionary was driven back to his native town. He raised the seminary of Coutances from its ruins, and governed it most efficiently; but as soon as the Company of Jesus was restored, in 1814, he abandoned his post at Coutances and hastened to Paris to solicit admission to the Society. After he had taken his first vows he was nominated to the important duties of Master of Novices; and thenceforward, for twelve years, from 1818 to 1830, during which time he was settled in Paris, he exercised the duties of his sacred ministry with unflagging zeal, and glowing charity that embraced all classes of society. Following the counsel of the Apostle Paul, he became all things to all men, that he might win them for Jesus Christ. The poor were the objects of his special preference; his compassionate heart forbade him to behold wretchedness without longing to assuage it, and instantly seeking for the means of doing so. " He was," says Père Guidée, "a man of strong and practical faith; most wise in counsel; a director deeply skilled in the ways of God, always simple, upright, and pleasing. His gay and affable manners charmed every one who approached him, and his goodness and obligingness won all hearts."

To this portrait, which is an exact resemblance, we may add the testimony of a priest who knew him intimately :—

"I do not know that I can say anything more than you already know about our good Père Roger. I shall always recall his wise advice with gratitude and affection, and never cease to bless Divine Providence for having placed me in relations with him. During my retreats he frequently said things to me which came like flashes of celestial light to my soul.

"It seems to me that I can still see him, coming to me in the evening, after a long day's work, giving way to his natural light-heartedness, saying the kindest things to cheer me up, and then, taking his seat in his arm-chair, and talking to me about God with such faith, simplicity, and love as I have never seen in any other person. What faith he had! . . . If Saint Paul desired to know nothing but the Cross, Père Roger wished to know nothing but the *Credo*. What simplicity also! 'Go straight to Almighty God, by the shortest possible way,' was his maxim. What love of Jesus! What a clear insight into His mysteries! Many a time have I seen him shed tears when he spoke of Jesus, whom he loved so much. Many a time have I thrown myself at the foot of my crucifix after an interview with him. And then, with what holy freedom he spoke to the great, and to all worldly people, not flattering words, but the truth which enlightens and saves. Never had any one greater skill than his in touching hearts, so that they opened themselves to him, and were won for Jesus Christ.

"It cannot have been without many struggles with himself that Père Roger had attained to the perfect amiability of character, and evenness of temper, that everybody recognised and admired in him; for his natural temperament was quick and fiery. He was always ready to listen to every one who needed the help, the instruction, or the consolation that his words were certain to convey. It would be impossible to describe the tone in which he used to speak of the mercifulness of our Divine Lord. Never can I forget the expression with which I heard him say to a person who was troubled by an excessive dread of receiving Holy Communion:—'But, my good child, what has Jesus done to you that you should be so much afraid of Him?"

"His compassion for all who were in any kind of trouble or suffering, his ardent desire to come to their assistance, endeared him to everybody. Who could ever tell how much the good Père Roger was loved and revered by the working classes, by the poor, and by children."

Immediately after she became acquainted with him the Duchesse de Doudeauville selected Père Roger for her Confessor. Her soul was refreshed by the strength and unction of the counsel which came to her from a heart in which the love of God was always burning like a flame. The kind of spirituality she found in him responded to the attraction she had always felt towards the hidden life; so that she consulted this wise director in all her undertakings, and he, on his side, held his penitent in the highest esteem.

Very shortly after the Duchess had placed herself under the direction of Père Roger, she was led by a providential coincidence to form an intimacy, which began with the relations of society, but extended to those of good works, with Mademoiselle Elisa Rollat, who was destined to be the first Superioress of Nazareth. The two ladies became strongly attached. Though their respective dispositions were widely dissimilar, they had marked features of resemblance : among these were ardent piety, love of duty, desire of perfection, and zeal for the good of all. They eagerly sought each other's society ; but the perfect tact of Mademoiselle Elisa Rollat prevented her from overstepping the bounds of deference towards the age and the position of her venerable friend, even in the closest intimacy. The Duchess, who greatly esteemed and admired her, reposed absolute confidence in her, and took especial pleasure in the bright gaiety under which lay a deep and serious mind. In talking with her the Duchess put no restraint on the utterances of her faith and her piety, for she was always certain of finding entire conformity of feeling in her friend. When they respectively left Paris for the country, a regular correspondence was carried on between them. A few passages from the letters of the Duchess will help to complete the portrait which we have tried to present; they reveal much of the habitual purpose and attitude of her mind:—

"I leave on Thursday, and am sad at absenting myself from the resources of which my weakness has such need. God is, however, everywhere, and He permits Himself to be found by all who seek for

Him in pure simplicity of heart; pray for me that I may meet Him where I am going. May He alone be our study; may His Divine Will encounter no obstacle in our souls, or at least none that His love shall not overcome. Such, my dear Elisa, are my earnest wishes for you; I intreat you to pray that they may be accomplished for myself—that will be much more difficult—but we must not be discouraged because things are not easy.

"Adieu! How much I shall miss your visits, and your reading to me; you have inspired me with a true friendship, one of those which does not find its close in this life."

Ten days later, the Duchess writes as follows:—

"Here I am in the most profound solitude; but it is to my taste, and I am very comfortable. As I am naturally fond of independence it must be very good for me to be always under subjection, and so perhaps it is because solitude restores my independence that it is so pleasant to me. However this may be, I enjoy it when God sends it to me; I wish I could make more profitable use of it; but I do not think I ought ever to seek it of my own accord; it would make me too happy.

"Zénaïde's letters are delightful; her children are charming. Yesterday little Alfred pronounced the name of God for the first time.

"My health has been very indifferent for the last fortnight, and so I am profoundly stupid. God wills it so, and I will it with Him. Let us, my dear Elisa, love this Divine will, for whose fulfilment our good Master came on earth.

"Adieu! It is at the foot of the cross that I desire to meet you; nevertheless, I am weak enough to wish that your cross should not be a heavy one."

Pére Roger was an additional bond of union between these two hearts; after he had made a short stay at Montmirail, we find the Duchess writing to her friend as follows:—

"I feel sure, dear Elisa, that you will be glad to have news of our friend. His health is better than it was when he arrived here. Everybody is charmed with him, and all recognise his talents, his eloquence, his high-mindedness, and the simplicity that combines with and completes those qualities. My son is perfectly delighted with him. M. de Doudeauville enjoyed his society very much, and my daughter-in-law took to him at once, and wanted him to remain here as long as she did. He has had, you see, a great success in our family circle, the success which sanctity and virtue will always have. He is so good, there is so much to gain by being with him! His ardent faith has made a great impression on me.

"The sacred songs you sent us are beautiful. Those on the Cross, Solitude, the Blessed Virgin, and the Love of God, have been sung frequently in the salon, to the satisfaction of everybody. If you could compose one on Trust in God, it would give myself and my daughter-in-law great pleasure.

"Let us seek God, my dear Elisa, let us seek Him with purity of heart, and love Him with all the capacity for loving that He has given us. Let us love Him in His greatness, but let this love be for His sake. Let us abandon ourselves to His good pleasure, and dwell in peace. This is what I desire for you as well as for myself, and I am not jealous because you will attain it sooner than I shall.

"Since you will have me write to you about my health, I must tell you that it has not been good, and perhaps I shall be obliged to come to a full stop for two or three days. To do enough without doing too much is a desirable point that I fear, with my nature, I shall never attain.

"Adieu, my dear Elisa, I forget myself when I am talking to you; which is another proof that I am not very mortified, but seek my own pleasure. This particular one is, however, permitted to us, as you know, and we must avail ourselves of it, provided always that we do so with the gratitude due to Him who has united our hearts in His love."

In her letters to her friend, the Duchess gave utterance to the pain which the departure of the Dames de la Paix inflicted on her; but on this, as on every other occasion, her faith overruled all else.

"Yesterday I received a letter from Madame de Saint Ambroise, in which, after six months' silence, she informs me that she is leaving for M——, with all her little colony. Thus, they are going away, with the savings of seventeen years, to found a house, and mine is left with its four bare walls, and the poor children without a mistress. God be praised! Thank Him for this fresh cross, and implore Him to make His will known to us. There are painful matters in all this, several things have hurt me very much, but as I have done nothing to bring about the occurrence, I look upon it as a decree of Heaven; I adore and hold my peace."

Shortly afterwards, the sorrow of the saintly Duchess began to change into joy; for she perceived that her friend might prove to be the foundation-stone that she was seeking.

"My dear Elisa," she writes, "your last letter—how good, and kind, and touching it is!—has given me a great deal to think about. Perhaps my imagination travels too fast and too far; however, it gives me hopes, which, if they ever be realised, will fulfil all our wishes. I shall be all the more happy in that case, because I shall have asked nothing, and the will of God will have manifested itself on behalf of an enterprise which has hitherto seemed to me a chimera."

The hopes of the Duchess were confirmed; the project of the new foundation became the common work of the friends. Père Roger, who was too busy to be able to write to her directly, sent advice and observations to the pious foundress, by the medium of Mademoiselle Elisa Rollat. The position was a delicate one, but the tact of the one and the excellence of the other smoothed away all difficulties.

"Once for all," writes the Duchess, "make your mind quite easy, my dear Elisa, nothing that you say to me can cause me any pain, I understand your motives too thoroughly for that; and besides, it is not in my character to attach importance to little things. When I am quite sure of a friend, she has a right to say what she pleases to me. What I ask for in your correspondence is confidence, candour, and simplicity. You give me satisfaction in all these respects, and you also re-assure me by your liveliness of mind. Why then should you take so many precautions about telling me that Père Roger considers I am going the wrong way to work with Mademoiselle C——? The contrary might have astonished me, but it is so natural to deceive myself!——

" Never be afraid of giving me pain on occasions of this kind."

Madame de Doudeauville, who was always ready to receive edification, and to do justice to real devotedness in the service of God, expresses the joy which she feels at the commencement of the work of Nazareth, in the following words :—

" I am most desirous to speak to you from time to time of our friendship, and yet I yield more and more to the necessity of discussing our business.

" Of course, Mademoiselle Mouroux keeps you informed of the satisfactory state of the house, but I am sure she does not tell you that she acquits herself of all the duties of her own position to perfection. She is overburthened—of that I have no doubt—for she sees to everything, and is always everywhere, but she never looks anxious or busy, her serenity is never disturbed. She is admirable indeed; the more I know of her, the more distinctly I recognise her valuable qualities, and thank Heaven for having sent her to us. She is sustained by the grace of God, and is of inestimable service to the children.

"Be easy, however, she has not the least notion that I think so highly of her. It certainly was my own project, but then, Père Roger had recommended it to me very strongly, as well."

These letters were written in the course of the years 1820 and 1821. While Providence was preparing the way of Mademoiselle Rollat, and disposing all things for the foundation of Nazareth, the saintly Duchess was once more called to the experience of the Cross. For some time she had felt that her sight was failing, and one day, while she was reading her prayers in the chapel at Montléan, a cloud seemed to pass before her eyes, and the printed lines of her book became confused. She closed the book, made an act of sacrifice, accepted all its consequences, and rejoined her family without showing any alarm, or grief. For two years she was obliged to refrain altogether from reading, and to use the greatest precaution in writing. In 1821, she became entirely blind, and refused, notwithstanding the entreaties of her husband, to submit to the operation for cataract; pleading her conviction that her blindness was the means by which Almighty God was withdrawing her from all worldly affairs. She knew well, though she did not say so, that blindness, by keeping her in perpetual dependence and subjection, would also hold her to the constant sacrifice of her own will. What an exercise of patience for a person of her active mind and habits, who was accustomed to transact all the affairs of her household and estates in person !

Those who witnessed her unruffled serenity cannot have conceived what it was to her to have to ask and wait for a guide; so happy was she to do the will of the Master, and to have one trait of likeness to Him. Were not His holy eyes veiled by a bandage on the day of His Passion? It was at this moment, when her need of her secretary and confidant was greatest, that she deprived herself of the services of Mademoiselle Thérèse for the benefit of the little boarding-school at Montléan. Without dwelling upon the extent of the inconvenience, she simply writes to Mademoiselle Elisa Rollat:—

"I shall miss Thérèse, on account of my infirmity; but one must not reckon up sacrifices."

The little foundation had become the chosen work of her heart; she occupied herself much with it, while she remained submissive to whatever it should please God to decide with respect to it. So perfect was her purity of intention that, notwithstanding her desire that capable persons should be induced to join in the project, she writes :—

"Mademoiselle C—— has formed a great friendship for me. We passed a week together, and I found her possessed of many fine qualities. She would be very useful to us, and as she had conceived an affection for me, it was plain to me that she regretted her first refusal. I perceived that she was endeavouring to lead me to say, 'You would give me pleasure if you would remain;' but as I did not consider that motive was one which would have the blessing of God upon it, I allowed her to go away.

"We still are in a great difficulty. To the eyes of reason we appear to be doing many foolish things, but how good it sometimes is to set that human reason entirely aside! Père Roger has prepared me to endure ridicule."

In 1822, Mademoiselle Elisa Rollat found herself at liberty, and the community at Montléan began to form itself. It would be a mistake to regard the pious Duchess as only the temporal founder of this little Society; she, who was filled with the spirit by which she desired to see it animated, had constantly practised those virtues which should distinguish the Ladies of Nazareth. Père Roger, though over-burthened with his own duties, and the charge of many important works, bestowed incessant care upon this little group, united in imitation of the laborious and hidden life of the Holy Family; but he devoted so much of his precious time to them, because he had been struck by the divine enlightenment of a soul whose piety had led him to exclaim, "I do not know how Almighty God will manage to send her for even twenty-four hours to Purgatory."

He was not unreasonably astonished that a woman of the world should entertain such correct notions of religious vocation; not only general ideas on the subject, but a distinct personal project. While the exterior plan was not yet sketched, she clearly discerned the object and the kind of perfection to be attained; one might say that the Holy Spirit had been prompting her from afar, for in her meditations she had always been drawn to contemplate the hidden life of Jesus at Nazareth. She had so constantly dwelt upon this subject in conversing with her children and grandchildren, that Mademoiselle Zénaïde had, of her own accord, brought her as a first specimen of her drawing a copy of the Holy Family by Carracci.

The child well knew how doubly welcome that gift would be. Another divine mystery also possessed a strong attraction for the Duchess; she went by turns from the Holy Child Jesus to Jesus on the Cross, and she would have wished to unite the two, so closely allied in her soul, in external form also. As, however, an educational establishment was in question, the name of Nazareth was preferred. Nazareth at the foot of the Cross; having the Cross for its foundation, its cradle, and its story.

The pious foundress was received at Montléan not only with respect and gratitude, but as one who brought aid of every description. Everything was explained to her, she was consulted on every point, requested to examine "subjects," and to pronounce upon difficult cases. She treated each question which was brought before her with equal wisdom and humility.

She knew all the nuns and all the pupils; she attentively watched the progress of her little pensioners, and interested herself in their future; she was both a mother and a saint to the children of Nazareth. When they had holidays, the Duchess would come, full of the kindliest interest, to encourage them at their play, and to preside over their little literary meetings. Her gentle gravity imposed no restraint, for no one understood better than she did that childhood needs a vent for its life and spirits.

The Duchess had inspired her husband with feelings of interest and affection towards the new community similar to her own. They were both of opinion that a school ought not to be situated close to an hospital, and that a chapel ought not to be used in common by pupils and patients, and they gave practical expression to these opinions by making fresh sacrifices. The Sisters of Charity were transferred, at the cost of the Duke and Duchess, to Montmirail, so that all the buildings and outbuildings of the old Priory at Montléan might be handed over to Nazareth. To this noble donation they added a rent-charge on the estate as a provision for the keeping up of the Society.

The relations of the community with the Duc de Doudeauville were exceedingly friendly and pleasant. He was as solicitous as the Duchess for the welfare of the establishment, and took every opportunity of proving his goodwill and kindly interest in it and in Mademoiselle Rollat. He encouraged the studies, distributed the prizes, and contrived all sorts of treats for the pupils. On each recurrence of St. Augustine's day he gave the school a splendid repast, doing the honours himself with that fine and urbane manner which distinguished him to the last day of his life. His kind patronage, his frequent presence, never gave the nuns the slightest trouble; he respected the rule not only of the community but of the school; always ascertained the hour at which a visit from him would be convenient, and arrived with exact punctuality. The Duke enhanced the value of the services which he constantly rendered to the little community by his perfect tact, and his ever active interest in their affairs was a source of great satisfaction to the Duchess.

The generous founders of Nazareth were always ready to come to its aid in the hour of difficulty. When, in 1830, Père Roger, being exiled from France, was trembling for the fate of the little religious household, deprived by the Revolution of all its resources, the Duchess came to his assistance like Providence itself.

He writes to her, renewing his injunctions, and reiterating his thanks:—

"Madame la Duchesse,—I was at Lyons when the terrible news came from Paris. All my anxiety was for you, and for our dear sister Rollat; from whom I am eagerly expecting news.

"Oh, how happy one is, at this present time, to possess a crucifix, and to know, as you have known so long, how to read in that ineffable book, so as to find there a sovereign remedy for the ills, the cares, and the afflictions that plunge one's poor soul into a sea of bitterness! Happy is she who lives by faith, and, while she quietly occupies herself with her domestic affairs, leaves the direction of the events that trouble and disturb the kingdoms of the earth, to Almighty God, for His own glory; she lives at peace in the midst of turmoil, and finds all her repose in the fulfilment of the Divine Will. The

Lord, always merciful and gracious, will keep under the sheltering wings of His providence His humble creatures who do not desire any other resource or asylum in the midst of trouble, danger, and alarm, than the Sacred Heart of Jesus. I rejoice to know that these are the sentiments of our good sister Rollat, and that you are of the same mind with her! How happy it would make me to be with you both! Rest assured, Madame, that my heart is with you, and that I never cease to offer up both one and the other to the Lord."

When the terrible pestilence of 1832 began its ravages, the good priest wrote to the Duchess, in the following strengthening and encouraging words:—

"I am sufficiently well acquainted with your sentiments, Madame, to feel assured that, although you are surrounded by the present epidemic malady, you are not bereft of either peace of mind or tranquillity of heart. You are too perfectly resigned to the will of God to desire that anything should be otherwise than as He wills it. Besides, He does not require the cholera as a means of depriving us of the life which He has given, and whose Master He is. Let us live in peace, and without the least solicitude; impress this on Madame Rollat. I would not that to any of my daughters the reproach of our Lord to St. Peter should be addressed : ' O thou of little faith ! Wherefore didst thou doubt ? '

" Self-renunciation ! Be that your watchword, and, above all, no belief in the multitude of prophecies which are disturbing people's mind, setting their imaginations to work, and hindering each individual from doing that which Almighty God requires from him personally.

" May God preserve you, Madame, for

the welfare of your own family, and that which is yours by adoption; and may it be granted to me to see you again, and to continue in concert with you the excellent work we have undertaken."

Very soon, however, alarm laid hold on Père Roger himself, and we find the consoler needing consolation and assurance in his turn.

"Since I last wrote to you, Madame la Duchesse, I have been exceedingly and increasingly uneasy, and I am in urgent need of news of you, your excellent family, and our dear house of Nazareth. I must acknowledge to you that my soul is very sorrowful, and that the *Alleluia* has failed to arouse any sense of joy in it. In addition to my pain and grief of soul, I am full of fears, of anguish, and of suspense, thinking of you in the midst of such danger as you must be exposed to from the scourge which is ravaging Paris, and remembering all who are so dear to me, especially our sister of Nazareth and her children. Now, indeed, are we in reality carrying the Cross, and made to feel its weight. Let us constantly repeat our Lord's prayer in the Garden on the Mount of Olives. Let me, however, beg that you will have the charity to alleviate my troubles by making yours known to me; I would rather know them than be left in ignorance, and I hope that I shall be given grace to resign myself to the blessed will of God."

At length, after much trouble and many sufferings, Père Roger and Madame Rollat had the happiness of meeting again. The Duchess was, however, absent from Montmirail, and Père Roger, wishing that she should have her share in the general rejoicing, writes to her as follows :—

"Madame la Duchesse,—You have

already learned from Madame Rollat's letters how kindly I have been received on my arrival at Montmirail by every one, even the town's people, but especially by the family of Nazareth, who, without distinction of persons, or ranks, came in a body into the courtyard to meet me, and expressed their joy on seeing me in so sweet, respectful, and reserved a manner, that I recognised the peace of the Spirit of God in it, and was deeply touched and edified. What a consolation it is for a father to see his dear children in the Lord again after a long absence! . . . The following day was celebrated, as was proper, by a solemn mass in honour of Saint Joseph, and by all the merriment and freedom of a whole holiday. May all the good that you have done to this dear house be amply repaid to you, Madame la Duchesse, and to your excellent family!"

CHAPTER IX.

FAMILY HOPES AND SORROWS.

Whilst the Duchesse de Doudeauville was passing her life in the exercise of those virtues which rendered it a "sweet savour of holiness" to all who witnessed it or were brought into contact with it, her husband was devoting himself to his unhappy country. Throughout all the political disturbances that had occurred since the Duke's return from exile, he had persevered in a course which had the interests of France and the cause of the unfortunate for its motive and aim. He filled, by turns, and sometimes simultaneously, the offices of President of the General Council of the Navy, and

Chairman of the Committee of Primary Instruction of the Seine; he sat in the Chamber of Peers, and was one of the administrators of the hospitals of Paris, and the State Institution for the Deaf and Dumb. In addition to all these duties, he devoted himself to the solace of every description of want and suffering; and was the vigilant and untiring benefactor of the poor, of the aged, and of orphan children. In 1821, he was made Post-Master General, afterwards he became a Minister of State, and a Member of the Privy Council, and in 1824, Comptroller of the King's Household. The latter post was peculiarly suitable to his character and congenial to his feelings, for it enabled him to procure assistance for numbers of unfortunate persons. Among the numerous occupations—every one involving the interests of the people—that absorbed his time, he imposed one in particular upon himself; it was invariably presiding when the requests of poor petitioners were to be examined. On a certain occasion a friend who perceived that he was suffering from feverish exhaustion, urged him to relinquish his attendance on that one day. He replied, "It is by no means indispensable that my health should be preserved, but it is indispensable that these poor people be not kept waiting."

In the inexhaustible kindness of the Duc de Doudeauville, there was, however, no touch of weakness; he was deeply solicitous to serve and to oblige, but never at the expense of his firm, upright, and enlightened conscience. He rated the demands of education at a very high standard, and felt the weight of his own responsibility in this matter. A portion of his charge was the governorship of the King's pages, and on one occasion it came to his knowledge that certain newly-arrived pages were in danger from the bad example of those of longer standing. On the spot, without any consideration of great names or court influence, he dismissed the boys, and he persisted in this rigorous measure, remaining equally deaf to all entreaties, and even to threats of the royal displeasure. He records his interview with Charles X., . as follows:—

"The King sent for me the next day, and asked me:—

"'Duc de Doudeauville, what is this you did yesterday?'

"'My duty, Sire.'

"'You have been terribly severe.'

"'I have only been just.'

"'You have ruined five interesting boys.'

"'I have only punished them according

to their deserts, and besides, I have done it with every precaution.'

"'What severity, for mere jests!'

"'Jests, Sire!—Jests that corrupt youth, poison schools, and form the misery of parents.'

"'At least you ought to have let me know.'

"'I had no time to do so; there was not a moment to lose, and my responsibility was seriously compromised, as well as the morals of the good and innocent children who had been entrusted to my care.'

"'If you had told me about it, I should have said to the parents, "Your children are behaving very ill, and if they do not alter their conduct within a month, I shall dismiss them."'

"'Ah! your Majesty will think me too bold, perhaps, but I congratulate myself heartily that I said nothing to your

Majesty about it. If I had done so, my good young people would have been ruined, and the department as well.'

"'Well, well; if anything of the kind should happen again, come and tell me before you take any steps.'

"'Sire,' I answered, bending low, 'it is my duty before all things to obey your Majesty; so now, it is understood that when the house is on fire, I am to ask your leave to put it out.'

"The King was not at all annoyed by my answer," adds the writer.

The Duke thought proper to resign his ministerial office some time before the Revolution of 1830. Although he had retired from public affairs, he did not relinquish his active zeal on behalf of the poor and unfortunate, and both at Paris and at Montmirail, his time and his heart were shared between his works of charity and his grandchildren.

FAMILY HOPES AND SORROWS.

The death of the Abbé Legris-Duval has already been mentioned in connection with the departure of the Dames de la Paix from Montmirail. This dear friend of the family had fallen asleep in the Lord, in perfect peace, in 1819, deeply regretted, not only by the dwellers in the château, but also by the inhabitants of Montmirail. His piety, his meekness, and his charity had endeared the good Abbé to all who knew him.

He had promised the Duchess, on his deathbed, that he would plead with God for her son and daughter, who were much afflicted because no child had blessed their marriage. A short time after his death the Duchess wrote to Mademoiselle Rollat as follows:—

"For the first time in thirteen years the Vicomtesse tells us that she has the dearest of all hopes. My son and she are almost afraid to believe that it is so, but

I have perfect confidence. I entreat you to return thanks to Heaven, and to ask that the child may be endowed with fervent and fruitful faith. This is my prayer before all others, and God is too good to leave it unheard."

The hopes of the Duchess and her children were realised, and not only in this one instance. Within a few years the Vicomtesse de la Rochefoucauld became the happy mother of six children, who formed a fair crown of matronhood for her.

To the great satisfaction of the venerable Duchess, the education of these children was entrusted to M. Bernier, an excellent priest, who was fully capable of training his pupils as Christians and gentlemen. The two eldest, Stanislas and Sosthenes, gave ample promise from their earliest years of the excellence to which they subsequently attained.

The children passed a great deal of

their time at Montmirail, indeed all the spring and summer, and they were perfectly happy there. Duty and pleasure reigned at the château, and their grandmother looked forward each day with delight to the hour that brought the little ones to her. It was a touching sight to see them, when the signal for recreation had been given, crowding round her chair and kissing her venerable hand. The Duchess would smile upon them with the ineffable expression of maternal tenderness which her countenance always wore.

"Well, my children," she would say, "the Abbé has been telling you some pretty stories to-day, I am sure?"

"Oh yes, grandmother, such pretty stories, and such old ones, too. And the best of it is they are all quite true. Perhaps you don't know them; maybe you were not told them when you were little?"

"That is very likely. Suppose you tell them to me now?"

Then came the ever-new old stories of Adam and Eve, and of Abraham; and the grandmother would listen with the utmost attention and pleasure, while the little speaker would go through the narrative with plenty of gesticulation, and without omitting any of the details.

Madame de Doudeauville took a special interest in the education of the eldest girl, whose vigorous health and ardent nature rendered it impossible to foresee her premature death. There was such an exuberance of life about this child that her governess, much as she admired her manifold gifts, could hardly keep up with her activity of intellect and incessant craving for movement and novelty. Sometimes the Duchess would intervene, and it must have been curious to observe the influence of her sweet, calm face and manner over the impetuous ardour which she sought to quiet down, while giving it the aliment that it needed. Encouragement and reward were united in this case, in permission to join in the convent games. The eldest girl's name was Elizabeth, and after her came Marie, a child of angelic disposition, who was subsequently placed entirely under the care of her venerable grandmother. A very sad event led to this arrangement. In 1834, the mother of these charming children died a holy death. At the first intimation of danger, the Duchess hastened to Paris. When the patient was told that her mother had arrived, she asked—

"Which mother?"

"Madame de Doudeauville."

"Ah, she is the mother of my heart," said the Vicomtesse, and a ray of joy passed over her face. That sweet presence seemed to her a safeguard on the threshold of eternity.

After she had received the last sacraments, the Vicomtesse wished to give her blessing to each of her children, and she counted them. Finding that the number fell short by one, she called for the child. The good grandmother had the presence of mind to cross the hands of the dying woman on the head of one of the children whom she had already blessed, and thus to spare her the pain of knowing that her little darling was no more. While she was asking for the child on earth, he had preceded her to heaven and was calling her thither; having expired a few hours previously, in the little bed that his mother had had placed beside her own.

Sorrows now fell fast upon the saintly Duchess. In 1833 she had lost her son-in-law, the Marquis de Rastignac, who had not married a second time; in 1834, her daughter-in-law and a grandson died; in 1835, she had to mourn her sister, the Comtesse de Montesquiou, and a few days later, while her tears were still freshly flowing, her beloved granddaughter, Elizabeth, was carried off, in the midst of health and strength, by typhoid fever, at fifteen years of age.*

Each of these successive losses inflicted a fresh wound on a heart which remained constant to the ties of family affection while it belonged to God also and entirely. Père Roger, who knew how it was with the afflicted Duchess, wrote to her, like the true friend that he was, in the following strain of consolation :—

"MADAME LA DUCHESSE,—I unite myself with you in the presence of our Lord,

* Madame de Montmirail, the eccentric but estimable mother of the Duchesse de Doudeauville and the Comtesse de Montesquiou, died in Paris at the end of December 1824, in the eighty-eighth year of her age.

and with all the affection of my heart I share the sorrow of yours! You know well, by faith, that every cross is a gift from God, and that each brings to the resigned and submissive soul an outpouring of ineffable graces and blessings both for this life and for eternity. You know better than any one, Madame, what the Christian would become, if he had not that stay to lean on which St. John of the Cross calls the 'strong staff.' The Cross has saved the world; the Cross preserves it by training the elect; it is the daily bread of the just, the food of the true disciple of Jesus Christ. The more bitter and painful it is the more it resembles that which, for the love of us, our divine Lord and Master carried. The very sign of the Cross is a benediction; how much more is the reality of the Cross benediction itself! The oftener we are bound to it the happier we should esteem ourselves. I say no more, Madame, because there is no healing for the heart in any words of man; that is the work of the Spirit, the 'Comforter' who dwells within you."

The infirmities of age add their weight to that of the heart's griefs, and augment the merit of patience. Père Roger pointed out the advantages of this union of trials.

"I can easily conceive, Madame, that, although you are in the company of many who are dear to you, your soul feels itself in a desert place, unable to disclose or communicate itself. It has an interior language, which is not that of the day, and makes itself heard only when all around there is perfect silence. Oh, how eloquent is the secret speech of the heart in solitude! What unspeakable things it says for you to the Heart of Jesus!

"We must not complain of weakness,

of the diminution of our strength and activity; our bodies must tend towards the dust from whence they came, and whither they are returning, while our spirits should strive to raise themselves ever higher and higher towards that heaven which is their true home.

"Do not think, Madame, that you are growing old; think, rather, as I do; for I feel myself growing young. The nearer we draw to the end, the more vigour and joy we ought to show. Our great wretchedness ought not to burthen us; it is ours indeed, and our sole equipment, but it shall be all absorbed in the Divine Mercy through the merits of Jesus Christ, our sole resource and our only hope.

"We will not speak any more of a union of prayers, that has been understood between us for a long time.

"You know that I did not leave Paris the other day without seeing the two dear children, Stanislas and Sosthenes. I enclose a line for Mademoiselle Marie, whose dear little letter gave me great pleasure. Providence, having committed your beloved grandchild to your charge, will also give you all that may be needful for the development of her promising character, and for her confirmation in the love of goodness and piety. Let her be as gay and cheerful as possible."

The grandchild of the Duchess, of whom Père Roger speaks, and to whom he sent a little note in almost every letter, had been confided entirely to her grandmother since the death of the Vicomtesse de la Rochefoucauld. Père Roger heard her first confession, and whenever he had an opportunity he gave her catechetical instruction. So great was the influence of his lessons upon the child's conduct, that the good grandmother abridged her own conversation with the reverend father, in order that he might have more time to devote to Marie. In the chapel, and among the poor, the child took all her pleasure; almsgiving was her chief delight. When she was entering her tenth year, the Duchesse de Montmorency, her maternal grandmother, sent her, as a New Year's gift, a rich velvet pelisse lined with ermine, thinking she would be delighted with it; but when the box was opened at Montmirail, the child burst into tears. The bystanders were much surprised, and they pointed out to her the beauty and the value of the pelisse. Marie, however, answered, while her tears still flowed, "Of what use can that be to me. I have plenty of cloaks to keep me from the cold, but I have nothing to keep the poor from it. Ah! if my grandmother had only sent me the money this fur cost, instead, I could have done a great deal with it."

A great-grandson of the venerable Duchess, Georges de la Rochefoucauld, was brought up with Marie. The two children were nearly of the same age, and they were equally pious and charitable. They agreed perfectly, were much attached to one another, and in their play-time their great delight was to decorate the chapel. All the household of the château used to assemble in the salon and sing the "Noëls" at Christmas, for the pleasure of the two children. They were dear little companions for their good grandmother, who used to recall all her recollections of the past to amuse and instruct them. She had many tales to tell of the dreadful Revolution—tales full of terrible interest,—but in which she always made light of her own part, dwelling upon the share of her relatives, friends, and servants, and upon the action of Providence. She recounted the fears, the dangers, and the persecutions of those days; and among other stories she told the children how it had happened that one evening, during the famine, she was very sad, because she had only one egg to share between her two children—(Marie's father and Georges' grandmother, the Sosthenes and Ernestine of this narrative)—but that when the egg was broken there were two yolks in it, and so there was great rejoicing, for two yolks of eggs in those days meant a meal. The little listeners hung upon her words; she mingled short reflections with the stories—sayings which the children could understand—on the usefulness of knowing how to wait on one's self, of learning to be satisfied with a little, and of being prepared for any event which may arise.

The children would interrupt her with their exclamations:—" You saw all those horrid things, grandmother! . . . You had no servant! You suffered all that!"

We know what power contrasts have over the imagination of the young; the two children were all the more moved by the picture of the privations which their parents had endured that they could compare them with the comfort of their own home and its surroundings. Their indignation was strongly excited against the authors of these ills, against those who had caused the death of their kinsfolk,—thirteen members of the family of Le Rochefoucauld had fallen victims to the Revolution,—but their grandmother sought to calm those feelings by repeating with the Saviour on the cross, "They know not what they do," and would add humbly, " My children, if the good God had not sustained me, I should have done as much as they." While Marie, in her grave and gentle way, strove to comprehend how the person who was the representative of all goodness in her eyes ever could by any possibility have been so wicked, Georges, who was of a merrier turn, would smile slyly, and, taking advantage of his grandmother's blindness, make signs to the other listeners that he did not believe a word of it. The Duchess would proceed with her narrative, and from time to time, when she came to the recital of some fresh crime, he would say quite seriously, "You would have been capable of doing just the same, would you not, grandmother?" Then, delighted to make her reiterate her act of humility, he would repeat his protestations of incredulity and his gestures of respect.

The antique château, which had been honoured by the prolonged residence of St. Vincent de Paul under its roof, received about this time another inmate, who was destined to be a future apostle and martyr of the faith. This was M. Olivaint, who, as tutor to Georges de la Rochefoucauld, commenced his beneficent mission.

The personal influence and persuasiveness that rendered the ministry of the zealous Jesuit so fruitful made themselves felt during his sojourn at Montmirail, where he was the soul of all the works of charity, and organised the Society of St. Vincent of Paul. Such a character could not fail to win the esteem and admiration of the pious Duchess, and M. Olivaint felt in her presence all the respect which is evoked by sanctity. Madame de Doudeauville was destined, to the end of her earthly life, to feed her saintliness at the fount of sacrifice. In 1839, the death of Père Roger deprived her, not only of a beloved friend and experienced guide, but of her most efficient helper in the foundation of Nazareth. If she did not tremble on that occasion for the future of the infant Society, she must have made a great act of faith. A fortnight before his death Père Roger had addressed the following letter to Madame de Doudeauville :—

"Madame la Duchesse,—I must make up to myself for having been so long a time without writing to you, but it would be difficult to say all I wish at the present moment. So many things come before one's mind at the end of a year and when another is just beginning. As there is nothing lasting in this lower world, and most men, and even Christians, seem to regard success in their temporal concerns as the only happiness that can befall them, I see but few persons who anticipate a year after their own hearts. Everybody seems to me to be dreading something. As for myself, although I am well aware that there are many causes for alarm and anxiety, I do not despair of a really 'good year' for myself, and confidently wish you one equally good. You, Madame, are so firmly established in the faith, and in the love of the Divine Will, that every event must needs be happy for you. What new benefit is the Holy Family preparing for us for this year? That is a secret; but be it what it may, it will be great, since it must be in the order of Providence, and for the good of your dear Nazareth."

The Duchess must indeed have learned to estimate events with other than the world's judgment, to bear, as she bore them, the successive trials which fell upon her. The year had opened with the death of Père Roger; the Feast of the Immaculate Conception witnessed the death of her beloved granddaughter, Marie de la

Rochefoucauld. The early piety of this dear child had been a constant source of consolation to the Duchess. A letter written by Madame Rollat contains most interesting details of the death of Marie, of a lingering malady, during which she greatly edified her family and all the household.

"Poor little Marie succumbed to her long illness on the eighth; she died as she lived, with the piety and the gentleness of an angel. Her happiness is not doubtful, not even her present happiness, nevertheless, pray, and have prayers said for her, for we know not the judgments of God. She received the Holy Viaticum twice, and Extreme Unction the day before her death, and she retained perfect consciousness to the last moment. She kissed a relic of the true Cross and a medal of the Blessed Virgin with the utmost tenderness. Shortly before her death a statue of our blessed Mother was placed near her bed; she looked at it with an ineffable smile, and then stretching her arms towards the sacred image, she cried out in an ecstasy, "Ah! how beautiful she is! . . . how beautiful she is!" Then, moving her lips in an effort to pronounce the name of Mary, she breathed her last sigh. Her face remained uncovered for twenty-four hours, and she continued to be as beautiful as an angel. She was taken first to the parish church, and then into ours, prior to her being laid in the family vault. Notwithstanding the weight of the lead coffin the congregation would not relinquish the consolation and privilege of carrying it themselves. All the inhabitants of Montmirail followed; we had to post guards at the doors of our chapel; the courtyard, and even the high road were crowded. The family did not wish that there should be any ceremony, the public mourning and the grief of the poor formed the most beautiful and touching one that could have been imagined.

"The Duchess bears her irreparable loss with admirable fortitude. Marie was the delight of her life and her habitual occupation; she stayed beside her bed until all was over, without shedding a tear, without the slightest sign of weakness; then, after she had prayed, she went down tranquilly to the chapel, heard Mass, and received Holy Communion. It was not until, on her return from the service, her two grandsons, Sosthenes and Stanislas, threw themselves into her arms, that she was able to weep."

The crown of sorrows came to the Duchess, when, on the 2nd of June 1841, Almighty God called the noble and pious Duc de Doudeauville to his reward. He had suffered severe and almost continuous pain for two years, and with heroic patience, employing the few brief intervals of relief allowed him by his disease, in caring for the poor and advancing the interests of the district. His fine face was changed by suffering, but his uprightness, self-devotion, and pious resignation had marked it with patriarchal grandeur; none could look at him without recognising a man who was great in goodness.

During the closing months of his life he was unable to go to the church, and the Bishop of Châlons authorised the chaplain of Nazareth to celebrate the Holy Sacrifice in the Duke's own apartment every Sunday. This was a favour which the Duke knew how to appreciate, for, in the midst of his gravest occupations, he had drawn up a list of the Benedictions given in the Paris churches, so that he might make sure of receiving the Benediction of the Blessed Sacrament every day in the week. He whom he had sedulously visited came to visit him in his turn, and he gave himself up to the blessedness of the Divine Presence, occupying himself no longer with the affairs of this world. On a certain occasion the Duchess came to tell him of the successful arrangement of an important family matter, about which he had formerly been anxious, but he stopped her gently, and said, "I do not wish to know anything more of the things of the earth." He received the last sacraments with fervent faith and joy. The entire population of Montmirail attended his funeral, and rendered homage to their generous benefactor.

CHAPTER X.

REPOSE IN GOD.

We are drawing near to the end of the long life in which fidelity increased with every trial, and love grew proportionably with fidelity. Ere we contemplate its calm and serene close, like the evening of a fine day, according to the promises of the Word of God, let us look on the following picture, which was drawn by the hand of a friend, and is preserved among the family memorials.

"In the old château at Montmirail dwells the octogenarian Duchess, regarded by all with profound reverence. Age has not altered her noble, striking, and regular features; it has but added to the majestic expression of her fine face; it has but replaced the charm of youth by that of grace and virtue.

"When strangers are admitted to the ancient residence of this noble race, they approach the lady of the house with unfeigned emotion; for all are aware of the purity and blamelessness of that long life which has been devoted to the fulfilment of every duty, and the practice of every virtue. They solicit the honour of touching with their lips that venerable hand which has never been stretched out except to give or to bless; that hand on which children and grandchildren press loving kisses. But their emotion is redoubled when they perceive that this token of respect and tenderness is the only sign whereby the Duchess can recognise her son and her grandchildren. That fair soul can no longer express its goodness and its loftiness by looks.

"But, though the once beautiful eyes of the Duchesse de Doudeauville can no longer see the light, her spiritual sight is bright and clear, and her intellectual faculties retain their youthful vigour. Gifted by nature as she was with ardent feelings and a lively imagination, her reasoning faculties were always so powerful that they kept those qualities under complete control.

"If she invariably treated all that was not perfectly pure, lofty, Christian, and upright with great severity, she never failed in extreme indulgence towards the sinner, whom she sought to rescue and restore, and all who needed such charity had an especial attraction for her.

"Her external demeanour is calm, but her words are full of warmth and persuasiveness when she is addressing those whom she loves, or is endeavouring to console the afflicted.

"She had great social success without having ever sought it; many admirers, without having deigned to accept their homage; she may perhaps have excited envy, but slander never dared to attack her. The excessive strictness which she practised in all respects towards herself did not prevent her from judging others with forbearing kindness. Who, then, would have wished to discover the weak point in so beautiful a character?

"All the powers of her mind, every faculty was concentrated on religion; to that religion she owed the teaching that has enabled her to walk firmly in the narrow way to the close of her godly life.

"Her heroic courage was put to terrible proof during the horrors of the Revolution, but neither threats nor peril could make her yield or take one step aside from the path of rectitude and honour. She wrung a reluctant tribute of admiration from the men who were on the point of sending her to the scaffold. The cruel sufferings that undermined her health had no power to shake her resignation.

"The Duchesse de Doudeauville has even more goodness of heart than gentleness of manner, and her feelings are profoundly tender, though she has none of what is called feminine sensibility. She never desired to shine in society, but in the domestic circle she is singularly charming.

"She likes serious reading, is alive to every lofty and generous sentiment, and is full of ready sympathy for every kind of sorrow and misfortune.

"Such is the Duchesse de Doudeauville, and certain points of contrast in her character, her mind, and her heart render her additionally attractive as an individual.

"May so bright an example for the edification of all be long spared to those who love and revere her."

These are noble lines, traced by a master hand, but we must read between them, and above all find the saint. We must never forget that faith and the love of God were the agents which set all the faculties of that fine nature in action, and that without them it might, like so many others, have wandered into vain theories and been beguiled into a barren life amid dreams of generosity and grandeur. The Duchess suffered much, but she did well in proportion to her sufferings. How many were her good works! How many were the souls saved through her means! What constant edification did she give to all who approached her! It might be truly said that every step of hers was marked by a benefit to some one. Let us not deceive ourselves, it is only God's grace that can accomplish such prodigies, and to have been kept thus to the end of her life, never once belying her calling, the model of duty and the apostle of love, she must have known what it was to draw in abundance from the source of holiness and infinite goodness. It was by means of prayer, constant, habitual, ceaseless prayer, that this admirable woman stored her soul with the treasures which she poured out on all around her. Prayer, union with God, perfect self-sacrifice, rendered her invincible. Thanks be to God, there is no stopping-point in the spiritual life, the soul mounts ever upwards, freeing itself more and more from the bonds of earth; and everything is a help towards this grand struggle whose merit grows in proportion to the efforts which the will has to make, and to the opposition that it experiences from nature.

The Duchess, being deprived of all power of action, henceforward lived in perfect submission of heart. She was condemned to physical helplessness, and she desired to preserve an attitude of continual dependence, not only on the Divine Will, but also on human aid.

Frequently, when she longed to hear the letters read that brought her news of her dear ones, did she repress that natural wish, and wait patiently until her secretary should come of her own accord to offer her services.

It was her custom to rise very early in the morning, and to go on foot, leaning on the arm of an old servant, to hear Mass daily at Montléan. In spite of the frequent expostulations of her grandchildren, and the invariable example of respectful deference towards the saintly Duchess set by them, the members of the household who were especially attached to her service, assumed a peremptory manner with her which she affected not to perceive, and which, indeed, she encouraged by her readiness to submit to everything that suited their convenience. It was not through any weakness that she acted thus. She never became familiar with her servants, and always maintained the most perfect dignity ; but she submitted in the spirit of mortification and humility.

A remarkable instance of her practice of voluntary humility was afforded by her prompt obedience when her old Marie would come to fetch the Duchess from the salon, and lead her to her room every evening at nine o'clock. One of the habitual visitors at the château, observing that she always rose at the sound of Marie's voice, made it a point on several successive evenings to turn the conversation on some very interesting subject, and contrived that it should be particularly animated just at the time when the good but somewhat rough attendant appeared. He never succeeded in detaining the Duchess, but just once he made her hesitate for a few seconds, long enough to give Marie time to say, "Madame la Duchesse, it is nine o'clock," twice over. As the saintly woman rose to follow the servant, she begged her to excuse the delay.

When she went to the convent, she asked that it might be made known to her when she had entered the corridor, in order that the rule of silence there might not be broken. Marie would convey the required warning by thumping her on the shoulder several times, but the venerable Duchess would never show the slightest sign of displeasure. So far from complaining of the members of her household, she never spoke of them except to praise their good qualities and their devotedness to her.

Her dress, though very simple, was always scrupulously neat; she would not have distressed any of the persons who were in the habit of seeing her, by the slightest departure from the rules of good society. Her great desire, nevertheless, was to economise in every possible way for the sake of the poor.

One day when, during a brief absence of her habitual counsellor, Mademoiselle Thérèse, she was visiting the convent, she asked the Superior, with the utmost simplicity, to tell her whether the gown she was wearing might not be mended again.

A poor woman, who was seriously ill, having run a long distance in order to reach a place which the Duchess's carriage would pass, so that she might tell her pitiable story, died of the over-exertion, and Madame de Doudeauville took charge of the three children who were left destitute by this terrible occurrence. She was so deeply affected by the circumstance, that, as she could not see for herself, she carefully inquired each time that she got into her carriage, whether any poor persons were standing about.

Towards the end of 1841, this venerable mother of Nazareth and of the poor was called upon to endure a severe trial, which caused the lustre of her charity to be more than ever conspicuous. For many years past she had handed over her revenues to her husband, reserving nothing for herself beyond a yearly sum for the expenses for her dress and the wages of her personal attendant. Out of this sum she used to take the alms of which she wished no trace to remain. To all the charitable works which the noble pair assisted publicly, the name of the Duc de Doudeauville was attached. "One is bound to set an example," he would say, "when one has fortune and a title."

The pious Duchess derived great happiness from seeing her husband thus following that counsel of the Apostle which says, "Let your light shine before men;" as in all that concerned herself personally, she preferred to practise the Divine Master's precept, "Let not your left hand know what your right hand doeth." Her favourite work of charity was the aid of the *pauvres honteux*.* When her husband jested with her on this point, she would merely smile, and glance towards the picture of the Holy Family.

During the years that followed the Revolution of 1830, the Duchess had witnessed the pecuniary difficulties of the House of Nazareth, which would have been unable to maintain itself if the Duke

---

* There is no exact English equivalent for this expression. It means those whose poverty is not apparent and acknowledged—the poverty of respectable persons, on whom it has come through misfortune or the death of relatives. The class is a large one everywhere. The succour of the "*pauvres honteux*," is among the organised charities of Parisian ladies.

had not largely assisted it on several occasions; and therefore, with her customary prudence and foresight, she wished to secure the means of existence to the community without entrenching in any way upon the family property. In order to do this she had placed her private savings, which she called her " reserve fund," in the hands of her man of business, and as she had pursued this course for some years, the sum was already considerable. The pious foundress of Nazareth allowed her mind to rest upon this increase as security for the future welfare of the community, and was quite happy about it, when, one day, this confidential agent arrived at Montmirail, and asked her to grant him a private interview. No sooner had Mademoiselle Thérèse left the room than M. L—— threw himself at the feet of the Duchess, and said, in a voice broken by his tears,—

"Madame la Duchesse, before I go to La Trappe, where my confessor has ordered me to end my days, I come to you, because it is impossible for me to repair the wrong I have done you, to entreat you to release me from the obligation of making restitution."

"What!" exclaimed the Duchess, "you have done me a wrong! Am I only concerned in it?"

"Yes, Madame, and I am deprived of the sacraments, and must remain so, unless, in your great generosity, you forgive me the entire debt."

"Rise, sir, rise quickly!" said the Duchess in great agitation; "I freely give you all that you have taken from me."

"But, Madame la Duchesse, it amounts to a considerable sum; all the money you entrusted to me as a reserve fund. I have gambled at the Bourse, and I have lost it all."

The unhappy man had just quitted the room, and his words were still sounding in the ears of the Duchess, who was profoundly troubled, when Mademoiselle Thérèse came in and was instantly struck by the change in her venerable friend's face. Her heightened colour, distorted countenance, and altered voice betrayed agitation which she vainly strove to conceal. Her trusted confidant questioned her closely and repeatedly, and at length the Duchess communicated the details of the scene, that had passed, to her. But she had no sooner done so than she was seized with a new emotion. "Thérèse!" she said, "I have done very wrong; I have acted unkindly; I assured M. L—— that I remitted his debt, that I freely forgave him. I had no right to disclose his fault to any one. Promise me that you will never speak of it."

Mademoiselle Thérèse was obliged to

make the required promise, in order to calm the troubled conscience of the Duchess; but she, notwithstanding her friend's assurance, repeated several times, "My God! I do not know how to imitate Thee; it is but ungenerous forgiveness that reveals the pardoned fault!"

She was, nevertheless, relieved by this avowal to her faithful companion, and she took immediate measures to secure the reputation of her treacherous agent from suspicion. She sent for him again, and made him destroy every record among his accounts of the sum which he had lost. She informed him that it had been her intention to endow Nazareth, and expressed the pain which it gave her to find herself henceforth reduced to the impossibility of doing so; and she demanded of him, as the only reparation of his guilt, that he should tell Madame Rollat what had passed.

"It is Nazareth you have wronged," said the Duchess; "it is to Nazareth that you ought to give, in future, all that is not absolutely necessary for your mother and yourself." Then, regarding this action as merely a passing temptation,—a fault committed in a moment of surprise—the Duchess requested M. L—— to continue to transact her business, and doubled his salary in consideration of the increase of his responsibility consequent on the death of the Duc de Doudeauville.

The required avowal was duly made to Madame Rollat, who was then seriously ill. M. L—— having asked, in the name of the revered foundress, for a private interview with the Superior, the infirmarian was dismissed, and Madame Rollat received the visitor alone. The visitation must have been a severe blow to the first Superior of Nazareth; but after M. L—— had left the convent, she

betrayed no sign that anything unusual
had occurred; no one belonging to the
house ever heard her utter a word in
relation to this grave matter, and the
secret, having been faithfully kept by its
three depositaries, would have been buried
with them in the grave, had not the unfortunate offender again betrayed his trust
and then made a declaration of his former
guilt and the generous pardon that had
been granted to him.

When Madame de Doudeauville beheld
the entire resignation and the imperturbable confidence of Madame Rollat, no
doubt she was enabled to find consolation
for the loss that had befallen her more
readily, and, with the Superior, to place
the temporal future of Nazareth, which
she had been so anxious to secure, more
entirely in the hands of Providence.

Shortly after these events, Almighty
God demanded a last sacrifice from His

devoted servant. It became necessary to tell her that Madame Rollat's illness was incurable, and she hastened to return to Montmirail at the beginning of April 1848, that she might have some final interviews with her. The holy friendship which had so long subsisted between these pious women had grown up in their community of labour and of suffering; their souls were closely linked by trial, by self-immolation, by supernatural insight; and the venerable Duchess was profoundly grieved when the moment of the great separation came. She was, however, much attached to the work of Nazareth itself, and she continued to give it constant proofs of her maternal kindness, occupying herself with the little society, it may almost be said, to her last hour.

Her strength was now failing rapidly. Her hearing became affected, she walked with great difficulty; the exterior life was fading by degrees, but the life of the soul was brightening daily.

She felt that the activity of her intellect was also becoming impaired, and prepared herself to accept this additional trial. She said one day, "I have made my sacrifice; let all be as our good God pleases."

Shortly after this she became ill, a slight attack of apoplexy reduced her to a state of complete physical exhaustion. As she sat in her arm-chair almost motionless, it might have been supposed that her mind had also sunk into apathy; but when God, her children, or Nazareth were spoken of, the life within sprung up again, and she would reply with a smile and an exclamation which revealed the vitality of her intelligence and of her feelings.

Père Varin came frequently to hear her confession and give her Holy Communion.

One day as he was about to leave the château, having fulfilled his sacred ministry, the Duchesse de la Rochefoucauld (the little Zénaïde of other days) detained him, and showing him a book relating to the Ecstatica of the Tyrol, she asked him what he thought of these stories, and whether they were not very wonderful?

"Madame," he answered, "the wonder of wonders, to my mind, is to see that woman of eighty, whose life has been full of every sort of trial, ready to appear before God, in her baptismal innocence."

The time came when the aged saint and the aged priest could no longer make their voices mutually audible; and then Père Varin had to be replaced by Père Lefebvre. As the Duchess did not evince any regret at this change, those about her thought that she had hardly noticed it, and that she was not aware that a longer interval was now placed between her communions, which were reduced to one a week. But the Superior of Nazareth, passing through Paris while on a journey, went to see Madame de Doudeauville, and told her that Père Varin, whom she had just seen, would very shortly pay his revered penitent a visit. What was the surprise of all present to see the aged lady lift up her clasped hands, and to hear her say in an agitated voice, and with tears in her eyes, "Oh, perhaps he will allow me frequent communion again!" They all deeply regretted that they had not divined the suffering of such a privation to that patient soul, and Père Lefebvre was entreated to grant more frequently to the dying saint the God of her heart, her life, and her consolation.

A few days before her death she seemed to revive, her strength rallied, and her family hoped that she was to be left a little longer with them; but she knew better. She felt that her end was near, asked for the last sacraments, and, as a preparation, begged that the evening prayers might be said aloud. This was done, and she, perceiving that a prayer for the Holy Father which she was in the habit of saying every evening, had been omitted, requested that it should be said. Père de Ponlevoy, who was present at the administration of Extreme Unction, repeated the prayers for the departing, in which the dying Duchess joined with fervour by signs and gestures.

Her children stood around her, hoping for a word, a sign of love. The Duchesse de la Rochefoucauld, bending over her, said caressingly, "Mother, do you still love your Zénaïde?" There was no answer; hearing seemed to be gone. Having repeated the same question several times in vain, the Duchess bethought herself of asking,

"Mother, do you love the good God well?" A strongly enunciated "Yes" made all present understand that henceforth she wished to think of heaven only.

On the 24th of January 1849, she gently breathed her last at eleven o'clock at night, in her eighty-fifth year, in Paris. Her spirit, freeing itself without any struggle from its earthly prison-house, took its flight to the bosom of God, whom she had so much loved, but left its majestic impress upon its earthly vesture. A profound sense of reverence fell on all who were permitted to see the temple in which the Spirit of the Lord had dwelt for so long a time. Children and grandchildren, friends, and servants, wept around the form which their saint, their treasure, had quitted; but all murmured amid their tears, "Blesséd are the dead who die in the Lord!"

The revered remains were immediately

conveyed to Montmirail, and placed in the vault at Montléan by the side of those over whom she had watched so long here below. At the approach of the funeral procession, all the villages in the district were deserted by their inhabitants, who flocked to Montmirail; orphans, old men and women, whole families to whom the saintly Duchess had been an earthly providence, formed her glorious escort.

Monsigneur de Prilly, Bishop of Châlons, united his personal regret with the public mourning. His letter to the chaplain of Nazareth on this occasion is a short but eloquent funeral oration, with which our record of this admirable woman may fitly close:—

"My Dear Friend,—I write to you because I feel that they have great need of consolation at Montmirail after having lost the venerable and generous foundress

who was its pride and its ornament. If
she were not praying for us in heaven;
if she had not left us, together with her
honourable memory, the treasure of her
example, that loss would indeed be without remedy and irreparable: nothing
would be left for us but deep and bitter
desolation, and we should be excusable if
we gave way to utter despondency. But
let us take courage! Madame de Doudeauville is still in the midst of us
—she lives—she will always live, her
memory is eternal. Ah! if we be not
saints, nothing will have been wanting on
the part of God, and there will be no
excuse for us who have had such an example before our eyes for so long. It is
said, and I quite believe it, that when
the Bishop of Hermopolis spoke of the
Duchess, it was with tears of admiration
and reverence; he did not know how to
express the feelings inspired by the sanc-

tity and excellence of a person who was superior to all others whose virtues we esteem, and who set a lofty example in the world. This illustrious and admirable woman was elevated so high above her fellows that she seemed, one may say, to be of a nature different from that of the children of men. Through the action of heavenly grace, and her faithful correspondence with it, she was unique in every kind of virtue, in piety, in gentleness, in sweetness, in amiable and charming humility—in a word, in all those qualities which transform the poor children of Adam into angels, to make them in advance fit inhabitants of heaven.

"It is a great and inestimable favour when it pleases God to give such examples to the world. We ought to profit by them while we may, and not to lag behind after having seen to what a point we may raise ourselves, and how far we may advance in the path of holiness by constant effort, and the steady endeavour of every day.

"Many prayers will be offered for the Duchess at Nazareth and elsewhere, and this is well—it is a duty; but she must also be invoked. I shall not be surprised if miracles take place at her tomb. As for myself, I shall apply to her in all my troubles. She was a person of sound judgment, and a lady of good counsel. Louis XVIII. prized her advice highly, and with good reason, and he frequently consulted her. I shall do the same, and it will be well with me; for me she will be always living.

"The details of the funeral ceremonies have touched me deeply; those obsequies will not be forgotten. We shall recall the fervent farewell of the people of Montmirail to the illustrious lady, and the tears which fell upon the coffin that is to dwell with you until the morning of the resurrection. In it you possess a true relic;—may it be a protection to you! I will ask that favour of the saintly Duchess for you. Let us strive to become worthy of her favour by following her example.

"May the blessing of the Lord rest upon Montléan, upon that house, the work of her hands, which was so dear to her. May that valuable institution prosper and ever be a refuge and a school for holiness and virtue.

"The hearts of the daughters of Nazareth rest and rejoice in the remembrance of her whom Providence inspired to create their little Society.

"We who are so happy as to possess in her blessed memory at once our model and our encouragement, utter but one prayer beside that sacred spot on which admiration blends with gratitude.

"May she who here below was devoured by her zeal for the house of the Lord, and who is now pursuing her noble mission on high in heaven, intercede for us, so that the number of Christian women who shall walk in the radiant light of the faith throughout their lives may be increased, and may she obtain the grace of fidelity for the humble religious family whom she so piously and generously loved."

NOTES.

Note 1.—*Page* 47.

In 1781, after his second marriage with the Princess of Wurtemberg, Paul the First travelled in Poland, Austria, Italy, Holland, and France, under the title of Comte du Nord.

Note 2.—*Page* 140.

The Abbé de Thiollaz was made Bishop of Annécy in 1823, when that city was raised to the dignity of an Episcopal see. He had been for many years Vicar-General at Chambéry, and was sixty years old when he was elevated to the Episcopate. He died on the 14th March 1832, and was regarded as a Confessor of the Faith, in consequence of the persecution which he had undergone during the Revolution.

Note 3.—*Page* 274.

"Mademoiselle Thérèse," as the venerable lady is called by everybody at Montmirail, is still living, and in complete possession of her faculties. She occupies a pavilion in the beautiful park which surrounds the château, and is the object of unceasing and respectful solicitude on the part of its present noble owners.

Note 4.—*Page* 293.

Among the most valued objects in the possession of the Convent of Nazareth, at Montléan, are several beautiful specimens of needlework executed by the foundress. These are preserved with the utmost care, together with some pieces of tapestry worked by Marie Thérèse of France, Duchesse d'Angouléme, who visited the Duchesse de Doudeauville at the Château de Montmirail, and took an especial interest in the convent and its pupils. The daughter of Marie Antoinette presented to the Duchess a court-mantle of white brocade, magnificently embroidered in gold, which had belonged to her august and ill-fated mother. It has been transformed into vestments, which are used on festival occasions by the Almoner of Nazareth. At the Château de Montmirail the great *salon* is preserved in precisely the same order as during the lifetime of the saintly Duchess, and the visitor is shewn the chairs, sofas, *tabourets*, and cushions embroidered by her. All are in perfect preservation.

NOTE 5.—*Page* 295.

The following are the verses addressed to his wife by the Duc de Doudeauville :—

> De vertus, d'agréments ornée,
> Sans aucune prétention,
> Ma femme a la tête tournée
> Par une fière passion.
>
> De travailler elle a la rage,
> C'est l'objet de tous ses désirs ;
> Toujours elle court à l'ouvrage,
> Comme un autre après les plaisirs.
>
> Au nom de toute la famille,
> Je dois l'arrêter sur ce *point ;*
> Trop souvent, de fil en aiguille,
> Nous le savons, on va bien loin !

Nous-mêmes, n'allons pas si vite
Et surtout ne condamnons point,
Ce n'est pas un petit mérite,
De bien broder au *petit point*.

J'y découvre de la sagesse,
Car en tous *points* que ne fait pas
Celle qui sait avec adresse,
Se servir d'un bon *canevas ?*

Dans le moins aisé des ouvrages,
Celui d'unir tous les suffrages,
Ma femme, sans peine et sans soins
A su réussir en tous *points*.

Je conçois que son talent brille,
Et son goût en fait *d'ornement*.
De son sexe et de sa famille
Elle-même l'est constamment.

Si tout nous plaît dans sa personne,
Tout est parfait dans ses travaux.
Elle est aussi sage que bonne,
Et je cherche en vain ses défauts.

Malgré mon goût pour la satire,
Son *point* de prédilection,
Je suis obligé de le dire,
Est le *point* de . . . perfection.

www.ingramcontent.com/pod-product-compliance
Lightning Source LLC
Chambersburg PA
CBHW051725300426
44115CB00007B/470